THE ART OF CONNECTING

Authentic
LIFESTYLE

THE ART OF CONNECTING

CONTENTS

5   **Foreword**
         The rise of three story living

7   **Preface**
         A Parable

12 **Part 1: Your Story**
         Chapter 1: The 'E' Word
17   **Chapter 2:** The First Connection

43 **Part 2: Their Story**
         Chapter 3: Listen Don't Leap
57   **Chapter 4:** The Needs of a Storymaker

68 **Part 3: God's Story**
         Chapter 5: The Truth of the Story
87   **Chapter 6:** Just Do It!

92 **Three Story Question Time**

Acknowledgements

Roy Crowne thanks:

To all at Youth for Christ who have inspired, stimulated and challenged me in our Mission to take the good news relevantly to every young person. Thanks for the brainstorming around the issue of peer-to-peer evangelism that helped to shape this book. Thanks to Karen McIntyre for your hard work and input. Thanks to Angela for all your hard work. Thank you to my wife Florence – it doesn't get any better than you. To my sons, John and Michael, for helping me to see when I'm being a "sad" man and when I'm engaging effectively in your teenage world.

Bill Muir thanks:

All my friends at YFC and my family, Karen, Billy, Jamie and Allie.

'Never underestimate the value of a relationship.' Roy Crowne.

FOREWORD

THE RISE OF **THREE STORY LIVING**

The Art of Connecting is the story of 'Three Story Living'. It was a concept primarily conceived by Bill Muir, then Senior Vice President of Youth For Christ in the USA. Like me, he had, for a long time, been concerned that many people he encountered seemed to have difficulty sharing their faith.

Why do so many people have hang ups over evangelism? More to the point, why do so few people who follow Jesus actually talk to others about him?

In January 2002, Bill came to the UK for the YFC staff conference and we found ourselves exploring these questions together. It was the start of a journey that would develop into a philosophy with the potential to change lives. We began searching for something that would help people to confidently share their faith. It was soon revealed to us. In fact, the answer was simple. It was right before our eyes as we chatted together sharing our hopes, dreams and desires. We began to realise that the key would be found in relationships: everyday, ordinary interaction between friends. We began to explore the idea of moving away from the traditional steps and decisions we had so often preached, and looking, instead, towards storytelling. The concept of 'three story living' was born when we began to recognise that people communicate most naturally when they are exploring their own stories together; sharing their needs as, over time, they reveal more of themselves. In this setting, God's story—that of the relationship he longs for with each one of us—can be gently and sensitively unveiled. It can be explored and dipped into in a way that doesn't manipulate, doesn't push, doesn't demand a set series of responses. Everybody can be comfortable, because God's story, told through a friend's story can be credible, not least because a true friendship relationship is credible.

We realised that 'three story living' can be communicated in a simple diagram, using three circles to represent three stories. One is your story, the second is your friend's story, and the third is God's story. You are part of God's story, so your circle and God's circle immediately overlap. As your relationship with him grows, more of your circle is merged into God's. You come across many people in the course of your story and as a particular person becomes a 'friend', their circle starts to move towards yours, so that they overlap. All the time you are becoming more a part of God's circle you are inevitably drawing your friend's circle towards God's. Then, over a period of time, your friend's circle starts to move towards God's circle purely out of its own desire to see more of what it holds. This is 'three story evangelism'.

Then came a startling discovery. We saw that our so-called new philosophy wasn't that new after all. In fact, as we studied the Bible we realised that it spoke loud and clear of three story living. The Bible itself is a story, God's story, and it tells of many others who interacted with God's story. Jesus, no less, was a master of three story living. He was the one who really made a connection with a person and then turned that person so they connected with God.

By the end of 2002 Bill and I had shared our thoughts with our staff and had put together a teaching plan that would enable people to share Jesus in an authentic, relaxed, comfortable and powerful way. It worked. People were excited. They were relieved. They were challenged. They were changed. They began to understand that life is a series of connections and, in every connection, God can do something through you. Moreover the more he does in you, the more he does through you.

This book opens up the heart of three story living. It is called *The Art of Connecting*, because that's what three story living is. Our prayer is that it will change your life so that you see every connection as one given to you by God, that you may learn from it and grow in it. Let it help you to make life changing connections…between you and God, between you and your friends, between your friends and God. Do we dare to call that 'evangelism'?

Roy Crowne
National Director, Youth For Christ

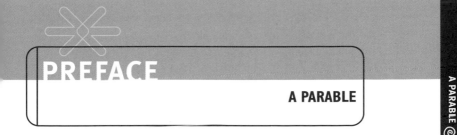

PREFACE

A PARABLE

When the storyteller's tale was over, a young man followed her away from the crowd. 'I was wondering', said the young man, 'if you might help me learn to tell the best and greatest story in the world?'

The storyteller stopped to look at him. 'And what is that story?' she asked.

The young man was confident. 'The story about Jesus,' he replied.

The storyteller smiled and stopped to rest on a stone nearby. 'Indeed, I believe that is the best story anyone ever heard and I would be very happy to help you tell it.' The young man sat at her feet as she continued. 'The first thing a storyteller must do is come to know his or her subject. How well do you know yours?'

The young man looked at the ground. 'That is why I am here', he said sadly. 'I struggle with what to say and when people ask questions, I cannot answer them.'

'I see,' said the storyteller. 'Then you must spend more time with your story. You must spend more time with Jesus. If you listen, in time you will learn his story by heart. When you have done that, come and find me again. Telling God's story hangs on three secrets, which I will teach you.'

A time passed, then one day the young man sought out the storyteller again. The old woman smiled when she saw him. 'So, do you know your subject better?' she asked.

The young man hesitated and said, 'I know more about him.'

'Good!' said the storyteller. 'You have begun the journey of a million miles. Continue on that path until you can say without hesitation that you are coming to know Jesus as a person knows an intimate friend.'

That is precisely what the young man did. The next time he caught up with the storyteller he was full of excitement and enthusiasm as he told her about his growing love for and friendship with Jesus.

'That's wonderful,' beamed the storyteller.
'Now, can you teach me the first secret?' asked the young man.

The old woman looked at him and smiled. 'You have learned the first secret yourself,' she said. 'Remember, the first thing a storyteller must do is come to know his subject. Your subject is Jesus.'

'Great!' the young man exclaimed. 'So now teach me the second secret. What do I say?'

'You don't say anything,' said the storyteller. The second secret is just like the first. You spent time with Jesus to learn his story. Now you must spend time with others to hear their story.'

'But I don't want to hear their stories,' protested the young man. 'I want them to hear God's story.'

'They will, my young friend, they will. All in good time. Now trust me,' she said. 'Go and listen, then return and tell me what you hear.'

The young man was frustrated, but he left and did as the old woman had told him. After a season, he sought her company again. 'What have you heard?' the storyteller asked.

'That it is difficult to hear people's stories,' he said. 'That people are slow to be honest. They are ashamed and afraid and hide behind masks.'

'Then you must unlock the places where people hide,' the storyteller said.

'And where is the key?'

The storyteller took the young man's hand and looked into his eyes. 'The key that unlocks their true stories is hidden in your true story,' she said. The young man was puzzled. He pondered on what she had said for a long while as they walked. Then, tentatively he asked, 'How much must I tell?'

'As much as it takes,' the storyteller replied. 'Some day you will meet someone who requires all of it.' They walked a while further, then she stopped and said to him, 'Learn to be generous and fearless. Speak the truth in love. You will learn when enough is enough.'

The young man was different when he returned. He was more humble and yet had a striking confidence about him.

'What have you learned?' the storyteller asked.

'Much,' the young man replied. 'I have realised that I too hide behind a mask of half truth, that I only reveal to people what I want them to see. I've also learned that my need for Jesus is as real today as it has ever been. Beyond that, I've learned that listening to another person's story with my heart and fully disclosing my own story in return, helps that person make space for God's story.

'That is a very good lesson', smiled the storyteller, 'And a hard one.'

'I had no idea how proud I was', said the young man, 'how afraid, arrogant, judgmental, ungrateful.'

The storyteller nodded. 'The one who is forgiven much, loves much.'

'I pray that some day I will love as much as I am forgiven,' the young man said.

'Then you are truly coming to know Jesus,' she said, 'and yourself as well.'

'So now will you tell me the third secret of storytelling?' asked the young man. The storyteller smiled. 'That part is showing how Jesus' story connects to someone else's story. That is why a good storyteller knows both stories well: that of Jesus and that of the person they are talking to. Go and see if you can connect the stories. Remember to share your story through theirs. Theirs will be quite different to yours. Always start with them.

The young man came back some time later.

'I see how Jesus meets people where they are,' he reported. 'I see how he connects with a person's need, often in a quite different way to how he connects with me. I had assumed that every person must be drawn in the same way', he said. 'But I never realised how self-absorbed I am until now.'

'What more?' asked the storyteller.

'Once I began to listen sincerely, my heart was broken yet again for those around me. I came to see my friends as sheep without a shepherd. And I could not help telling them how Jesus came into my helplessness, how he shepherds me still and will shepherd them if they wish it.'

'And do they wish it?' the storyteller asked.

'They do indeed,' the young man replied. 'Not all, but many, and with all their hearts! As for those who do not yet wish to know Jesus as I do, I am committed to my relationship with them, to know them more. Above all, I am committed to my relationship with Jesus, to know him ever better and I believe that my continuing relationship with him will help me understand what part of God's story most graciously connects my friends with Jesus. In the meantime, I will feed the fruit of God's story in their lives.'

'Great!' said the storyteller. 'You have learned the three secrets. Now go in peace.'

Seeing the storyteller's words were true, the young man returned home excited and eager to tell the story of Jesus as never before.

PART 1: YOUR STORY

CHAPTER I: **THE 'E' WORD**

Hi there, thanks for dropping in, I was hoping you would. Why don't you grab a Coke or something, chill out and let's just spend some time together. You'll be glad you did. In fact, I think this is going to be one of the most significant books you've ever read. And let's face it, it's not going to take long, but big things often come in small packages, and boy, have I got some big things to tell you.

 It all begins with a story. God's story. Like many good stories it starts, well, 'In the beginning...' Then there's the middle, where lots of stuff happens...everything you'd expect from a really gripping story. There are fights, feuds, romance, horror, passion, betrayal, and ultimately—after some really wacky stuff involving angels and spewing dragons—a happy ending. Somewhere in the middle of all that, my story starts. You'll discover a little of that as we go along and I'll introduce you to some of the friends that drop into my story from time to time. They also have their own stories and we'll be taking a peek into them through our 'talk back' sessions with John. Ah yes, John. He's our youth group leader. He's a cool guy and a great listener. He just seems to know stuff and he's always getting us to look for answers to our own questions. A lot of the time that involves digging through the Bible, which sometimes drives us crazy...but then he has an annoying habit of being right about things...

With me so far? Probably not. Well, hang in there because we're on a journey of discovery. First of all, I'll let you into a secret; that which is at the heart of this book, that which requires the 'art' that drives a 'connection'. Now if you read the next bit fast enough, it won't scare you so much. It's all about the 'e' word—evangelism. There, now, that didn't hurt did it?

Like it or not, if you're a follower of Christ, you're inevitably going to be an 'evangelist'. Oh yes, one morning you're going to wake up to discover you're wearing a white suit, a toothpaste ad grin, you're speaking with an American drawl and have a haircut that came out of the seventies (before retro was cool!). No, seriously, the very word 'evangelist' has some really dodgy connotations these days, but that's not what it's all about. Remember, I said if you're a follower of Christ—a 'Christian'—you're going to be an evangelist. That's not to say you're going to be stood up in your next school assembly preaching and waving your Bible around (though you might), but rather that what you have and what you know to be true is so exciting that you can't help but want to share it in some way. That's evangelism, pure and simple: sharing God's news, the 'Gospel'. In other words, 'communicating God's story'.

An obvious question then: Is evangelism important? (There's a clue in the fact that I've bothered to write this book and you're spending your time—so far at least—reading it.) Well, we don't even need to get too hung up on that one. Rather, just ask yourself, 'Is Jesus important to me?' Hopefully you jumped in with an emphatic, 'Yes, of course.' Perhaps, like many others, your answer is a more hesitant 'Yes, most of the time.' Either way, let's go ahead with the presumption that you know your life is better because you've heard about Jesus, you've recognised his sacrifice for you (even if this whole concept still blows your mind), you've asked him to be part of your journey and you have the expectation of eternal life, as he has promised. Well, I'd say that's pretty big and pretty important.

Another question then. If Jesus is that important to me, why do I find it so hard to share that news with others? Well, that's what this book is really all about. But let me get one thing straight. If you're looking for an easy formula or step by step guide to make someone become a Christian, you're not going to find it here. Truth is, I'm not convinced those formulas work, at least not today. After all, why should a person take notice of me, let alone trust me, if I corner them and push them through the four traditional evangelism steps. One: There is a God who loves you. Two: You have sinned and separated yourself from him. Three: Jesus died for you. Four: If you put your faith in him you will be forgiven. It will probably just get the response, 'Yeah, so what?!' By this time it will be conversation over, and your friends running for cover. This stuff is all true, of course, but there's something badly amiss with the method of communicating it. Somehow it doesn't connect on my wavelength. You neither, eh?

Remember I talked about stories? I'm convinced this is the key to really unlocking the 'e' word. So essentially we're going to be looking at how to share God's story by connecting it to our own. In turn we'll see how we connect our story to that of other people and, therefore, how their story can become part of God's story. If you like, we'll call it 'three story evangelism', or 'three story living', if we're more comfortable with that.

For now, I sense there's an interesting conversation going on at John's place...

TALK BACK

John: *Hi Emma, you look upset, what's the problem?*

Emma: *I'm beginning to feel guilty about this whole evangelism thing. We had great teaching on Sunday based on Matthew 28, where Jesus tells his disciples to go out and make followers in all the world. I know that's what I'm supposed to do, but I just don't know where to start. I feel ashamed. I've been a Christian for six years so it should be something I can do, but I can't even tell my friends, never mind try to preach to a stranger in another country.*

John: *Let's leave strangers and foreign lands out of this for a while and concentrate on your friends, the people you see day to day. Where do you think you should start with them?*

Emma: *Maybe by telling them Jesus died for them?*

John: *That's true of course, but it's not the kind of thing that easily comes up in conversation is it?*

Emma: *Exactly. And if I say that they're just going to think I'm some kind of religious freak.*

John: *So we need to find another starting place.*

Emma: *I guess so. Truth is, whatever I say, I'm scared it might all go wrong. And it's not exactly cool to say you believe in Jesus anyway.*

I always think they're going to ask questions that I can't answer? Y'know, like why bad things happen in the world, all the suffering, and what about the Adam and Eve story, and dinosaurs? Do I really believe God created the world in seven days? ...all that stuff...Half the time I don't know what I think myself, never mind being able to convince someone else.

John: *Chill out Emma. I do know what you mean. Let's have a look at some of the promises Jesus made to us though. Look up Matthew 6:33. Then, have a look at Romans 15:13.*

Emma: *What do they say?*

John: *If you look in the NCV Youth Bible, Matthew 6:33 says, 'The thing you should want most is God's kingdom and doing what God wants. Then all these other things you need will be given to you.' Then Paul, talking to the Romans says, 'I pray that the God who gives hope will fill you with much joy and peace while you trust in him. Then your hope will overflow by the power of the Holy Spirit.'*

Emma: *Yeah, but that doesn't solve my problem.*

John: *No, at least you may not instantly think so, but spend some time thinking about these verses and ask God to help you understand and apply them to yourself. These verses really help me get things into perspective and I suspect you'll find the same. They'll probably start to open up a new journey for you.*

Emma: *Hmmm. Thanks. I think.*

I may not be a preacher
  I may not be an evangelist
    I may not be a teacher, a prophet or a missionary
  I am a witness for Jesus
    I do live his Love
        Joy
          Peace
          Hope
          Light
  I do have a story

PART 1: YOUR STORY
CHAPTER 2: **THE FIRST CONNECTION**

Now, let's go back to where we started, with God's story. The crucial bit for the purpose of this book is the part where you and I come in, the bit in the middle where our stories collide with God's and hopefully intertwine in the way he intended. Now, bear in mind that God wrote us into his story in the first place and gave us everything we need to engage with him—to worship him as our Creator, to love him as our Father, to know him as our Saviour, to lean on him as our Helper, to serve him as our Lord. Easy to say this stuff eh? But in reality, how do we connect with Almighty God? It's not easy, but the truth is written in his story. Yes, God revealed something of himself when he sent his son to live on earth as a human being. When Jesus said 'I am the way, the truth and the life. The only way to the Father is through me.' (John 14:6), he was talking about making that all-important connection. And that's what the Gospel stories are all about—Jesus making connections with ordinary people, like you and me.

Ordinary, like me? Yes. Now stick with me on this, it's important. We know that Jesus was God's son, but what we must remember is that when he came to earth, he was truly human. Why do you suppose that after his birth we heard very little about him until he was a grown-up? Well, it's probably because he was just getting on with his ordinary human life: going to school, hanging out with his mates, enjoying a good laugh, all the usual stuff. As we read the Gospels we see him being truly human. He wept when his friend died, he got angry when he saw injustice, he loved to hang out with his friends, sharing food and telling stories. If he was sent to us today he'd be the kind of guy you'd love to be around. He'd laugh at your jokes and tell a few of his own, he'd send you text messages, play computer games, kick a football around and generally be a cool mate just doing every day things. Consider the people Jesus chose to spend time with. They came from all walks of life and Jesus was able to communicate with each individual, just in the way they needed. From the religious and influential, to the working people, the fishermen, tax collectors, prostitutes. They were people who, just like you and me, had needs. They might have lived a very different life to our twenty-first century existence, but they no doubt knew what it feels like to be lonely, confused, left out, angry, emotional, anxious, stressed…

So what's the point here? Well, the point is that when we relate to Jesus as totally human and understanding of our needs, no matter who we are and what our background, he becomes extremely interesting to us. When Jesus becomes a curious, complex and passionate person to me, he will, at the very least, engage the attention of my friends. The more real he is to me, the more real he becomes to those who know me. To know his story is to know the greatest story ever told. To understand that we can be part of his continuing story is more than appealing.

Lonely, confused, anxious, stressed?

God sent his son to live on earth so that he could fully understand and share in the difficult things we go through.

Read Hebrews 4:15.

Another thing we need to recognise, especially when we're feeling inadequate, is that the ordinary, largely uneducated people who hung around with Jesus were the ones given charge of the most precious story of all time. They were the ones who had the privilege of first sharing Jesus with others. The Bible gives us the amazing stories of the gifted evangelists Peter and Paul, but we can also be certain that there were hundreds of other witnesses, less celebrated, but equally important, who passed on the Gospel message, being storytellers or 'evangelists' in their own back yards. Guaranteed, the ones who were most effective at spreading the message of Jesus after his death and resurrection were the ones who knew him, the ones who had spent time with him, who sat at his feet, listened to his teaching, ate with him, laughed with him and enjoyed his company. They were convinced by him because they knew him.

Now, I think there's an interesting conversation going on back at John's...

TALK BACK

PART 1: YOUR STORY

Jason: I guess Emma told you what happened on Sunday. I think we were all pretty challenged by the preacher. It was a great meeting. The band were awesome! We sang this song, 'I'm not ashamed of the Gospel...' Anyway, I've decided I'm gonna go for it. Before you know it, all my friends are going to become Christians. I just need you to teach me how.

John: I would be happy to.

Jason: Great. When can we start?

John: How's your walk with Jesus?

Jason: Er, fine, but it's not about me, it's about them.

John: Them who?

Jason: My friends who don't know about Jesus. I already do.

John: You do?

Jason: Of course. I grew up in Sunday school. Heck, I teach Sunday school. I ought to know.

John: Yeah, but I believe that knowing him and knowing about him are two different things.

Jason: And again?

John: Well, it seems to me that telling God's story to friends is just as much about you, as it is about them. It all starts with you: who you are to them and, most of all, who Jesus is in you. Think about it. Is it knowing about Jesus, or believing in and following him that we're talking about here?

Jason: I think I see where you're heading, but I'm still not sure what to do about it.

John: The first question is, are you sure you want to do something about it? Remember, it has more to do with you, who you are and who you could be than you've probably bargained for. Are you prepared to discover that?

Jason: Now I really am intrigued. Where do we start?

John: Let's have a look at the Bible.

Jason: How did I know you were gonna say that!

John: Okay, make note of these references and check them out. See if you can apply what they're saying to your life: Matthew 5:13–15; 1 Peter 3:15; 1 Thessalonians 4:11. When you've looked at these, perhaps you could find some more parts of the Bible with the same message.

So how do we ensure Jesus is real to us and truly woven into our story, our life?

If we read the New Testament we learn that our first priority in life is to get connected to God, and second to get connected to others. 'Love the Lord your God with all your heart, all your soul, all your strength and all your mind. Also love your neighbour as you love yourself' (Luke 10:27).

Let's just pause to consider a useful analogy that Paul used in his teaching to the Hebrews. He talked about needing milk before solid food. Imagine if a parent tried to feed their newborn baby on chicken legs or hamburgers. It wouldn't be able to pick up the food, let alone chew it or digest it. Eventually, the baby would starve. No, what the baby needs in the first stages of life is milk. It needs to be gently nourished until the time when its stomach can cope with more solid food. Gradually, the parent should introduce soft food that can easily be swallowed and will not distress a fragile digestive system. A good while later, the baby will start to develop teeth and begin to be able to cope with something a little less sloppy. As time goes by, the baby will be able to help itself with the feeding process. It will be very messy, but the baby will begin to take the spoon from the parent and put it into its own mouth. All the time, the baby is growing stronger and developing in all sorts of ways.

That is the way it is with us and our relationship with God. We need to be totally reliant on him to feed us, to develop us, to grow us. During that time it may get messy, but he will be feeding and nourishing us and, gradually, we will begin to crave more and more solid food.

You see, when Jesus gives us the instruction in Luke 10 (about loving him and loving our neighbour), he doesn't expect us to do it in our own strength. We don't suddenly decide to put ourselves in a right relationship with God and 'wham!' everything is different. Rather, it is a process, and because we choose to let him be the source of our nourishment, he helps us to grow and develop in this way.

When our relationships are healthy and thriving on his nourishment we will have a quality of life that is not only fulfilling, but is attractive to others around us. As we read through this book, an important thing to grasp hold of is the recognition that God will always do as much in you as he does through you. Think about it then: the more you let him do in you, the more he will do through you for the others in your life.

So how, in reality, do we get to know Jesus this intimately? How do we learn to live with him in the ordinary, the extraordinary, the ups and the downs of our ongoing, ever developing story. It's not easy is it? We can hardly take him out for a pizza or call him on the phone, the way we would with any other friend. We can't actually sit and chat with him face to face. He is, essentially, invisible. Then again, if we believe what the Bible tells us, this needn't be a problem. Remember what Jesus said to his friend Thomas when he appeared to the disciples after his resurrection. 'You believe because you see me. Those who believe without seeing me will be truly happy' (John 20:29). That would be us. Peter also says of us, 'You have not seen Christ, but still you love him. So you are filled with a joy that cannot be explained, a joy full of glory' (1 Peter 1:8).

God reached out to 'connect' with us through his son Jesus.

We don't have to earn our way into his good books. Nothing we can do will make him love us more. Likewise, nothing we can do will make him love us less. That's the thing we call God's 'grace'. We need to realise this and to live in it!

Until our story on earth ends, our relationship with Jesus will always be based on faith, on believing that which is known in the heart, but not usually seen or felt in the physical. Hebrews 11 tells us, 'Faith means being sure of the things we hope for and knowing that something is real even if we do not see it.' And yet that faith is rewarded here on earth, as we do 'experience' God in our lives. Throughout our lives, there are moments when we just know that God is weaving the threads of our story; when we recognise beyond doubt that we are in alignment with his will. That's when we make a connection. If this all sounds a little random, don't be worried. Our big quest on this journey is to learn more of Jesus, and in doing so, let him transform us to become more like him. How do we do that? Well, we're certainly not left stumbling in the dark. Far from it. In fact, that's why God gave us the Holy Spirit to help us, to be our companion in our day-to-day lives. And be sure that, through the working of the Holy Spirit, God holds onto us far tighter than we could ever hold onto him!

God has also given us many tools to help us grow in knowledge, strength and intimacy with him. For now, we'll think of them as tools to help us 'connect'. Some might be more natural to you than others, and the ones

Rest assured, God holds onto us far tighter than we could ever hold onto him!

you find most helpful won't necessarily be the ones most enjoyed by your friends. Remember, your relationship with Jesus is not dependent on your actions. You are not required to 'earn' your way into heaven. However, your 'passion' for Jesus will be deepened as you use and practise with some of the 'tools' I'm about to talk about...

Tools of connection

Worship

Worship, by its very definition, can lead to the most intimate connection with God. Though it certainly does not have to be the case, many of us find that music plays a very important part in our worship. (Probably because it plays an important part in our lives.) Don't imagine that this is just a modern phenomenon since the appearance of the Martin Smith and Matt Redman song repertoire. Back in the Old Testament, David—perhaps the Bible's most famous worshipper—found himself connecting to God through music. The Psalms are full of emotion and the outpouring of David's heart. At times, when he was struggling, feeling life was really stacked against him, David knew that his singing of praises would lead him into a very precious and powerful encounter with God. There is something about music that can help us set our inhibitions aside and focus our hearts, minds and bodies on connecting with God. Honest, authentic worship requires brokenness and submission to God and it is not uncommon to find people experiencing healing or being given gifts of the Spirit through such intimate times of worship.

The great thing about worship is that the means and methods are limitless. It can be as deep and wide as our imagination. We might dance before the Lord, we might meditate using a lighted candle to focus our attention, we might join thousands of others in noisy rock-style celebration, we might create a piece of art...The most important thing is that we find a way that allows us to most freely express our love and passion for Jesus.

PART 1: YOUR STORY

I will worship alone, I will worship with others.
I will be loud, I will be quiet.
I will raise my arms, I will kneel before him.
I will tell God how wonderful he is,
How majestic he is,
How eternal he is,
How powerful he is,
How loving he is...
In worship I will take my eyes off me,
Off problems,
Off others,
Off disappointments.
My eyes will be on him.
I will discover him in praise.
I will play music that builds me,
That encourages me,
That cleans my head.
I will play music of those who sing of him
So that I too might sing of him.
My music will take me to the throne room, not the gutter.
It will raise my soul, not my flesh.
I will worship him in all things, through all circumstances,
with all that I am...

But also remember that authentic worship is a 'lifestyle'. Read Psalm 100: 2–4. If on a daily basis we 'Come into his presence with singing...enter his gates with thanksgiving and his courts with praise', such praise-filled open-ness to God will plant in us a deep devotion and a desire to practise more of the tools of connection we're going to look at. 'All well and good', you might say, 'but what about the days when I don't feel like singing or jumping about in joy and thanksgiving. What about when it's a rainy, grey day, when I've got lessons I don't enjoy, when I get a bad mark in my homework, when

✶ **Worship is our 'expression' of our love for Jesus.**

Worship him with music, with dancing, with laughter, in sorrow, with singing, in tears, with joy, with sadness, in pain, in pleasure...in all things. Worship him as you are.

I've argued with my brother and sister, when I feel mad at the world? What about when I walk into church on Sunday morning but I'd rather be at home in bed or watching TV? How is worship a "lifestyle" then?' Well, in all things, whether it's before our friends, or before God, it's most important that we are 'real'. So on days like this, there's just no point trying to pretend that all is well. Let's go back to David, the Psalmist again. A number of his psalms were written in a minor key. They were very painful, soul-searching laments. But God heard his cries. They were authentic. They were real expressions to the one he loved of the way he felt, even though that was lousy! And what happened? Well, David's spirits were lifted. As he drew close to God in the misery of his real feelings, God drew close to him and strengthened him. God connected to David in the hard times as well as the good. In fact, in those hard times he probably pulled him ever tighter. The book of James instructs us, 'Come near to God, and God will come near to you.' (James 4:8). That's when worship is a lifestyle, when it's real, when it's 'connected'.

The Bible

Much can be said about the importance of scripture. It is, after all, God's Word, his story and his instruction book for us. It's also been said that the Bible is God's love letter to us. Imagine if someone stuck a Bible through your door next Valentine's day! Weird idea? Maybe, but dip into many parts of the Bible with this in mind and you'll see what I mean. It's even there in the language. Check out the Song of Solomon and you'll find language to make you blush! Anyway, before you get any more hot and bothered, just think about this: Can you imagine loving someone enough to die for them? It's the stuff of the most tragic and romantic movies! So you see, to study scripture is to dig deep into God's heart, to explore his mysteries and get to know him as you read about him.

Let's face it though, most of us go through times when we find it difficult

The Bible is God's love letter to us.
It is also the best manual to show us how to live. God has given us the Holy Spirit to help us to read and understand it. So ask for his help. Ask him to speak to you through his Word as you grow to love it. (Read 2 Timothy 3:16–17)

PART 1: YOUR STORY

to read the Bible. That's why it can be a good idea to use some helpful notes or a guide. Often we can get more out of our study when it's done with another person. It's always easier when you can discuss what you're reading and get someone else's perspective on applying the scripture to your life. And, like all things, the best way to learn and understand is to memorise, so why not try to learn by heart some of your favourite and most inspiring passages. Above all, remember to involve God in your reading. Ask him to open up his story to you, to guide you and inspire you as you read. **It will make a difference.**

Don't think you have to read the Bible from beginning to end.

Start with the Gospels. Dip into the stories. Use Bible reading notes to help guide you, or study passages with another Christian friend or leader. Memorise passages so that you can treasure them deep in your heart.

I will discover God in the Scriptures:
In the ark, in the burning bush, in the tabernacle, in the temple, on the cross, in his kingdom.

The Bible is:
My user's guide, my map, my textbook, my information pack.

It will tell me:
How to live, how to love, what to say, how to go, what to value.

I will let it be:
Air in my lungs, light to my eyes, music to my ears, food for my soul.

I will think of it as mail that I can read:
In my bedroom, on the bus, in the park, at the coffee shop.

Yet the Bible isn't just another text message, or book, poem, novel or letter:

It's his message, his book, his poem,
his letter of love to me...

TALK BACK

PART 1: YOUR STORY ⊙

Andrew: I know what you're going to say John. You're going to tell me how important it is to have a daily time reading my Bible...

John: Hang on mate, let's slow down. Yes, I think it's cool if you can spend time reading your Bible every day, but not if it's a chore. Tell me a bit about the way you're struggling.

Andrew: Well, for the last five years I've made a New Year's resolution to read through the Bible.

John: What, the whole thing, starting at Genesis?

Andrew: Yes. Surely it's the best way to do it to get the full picture?

John: Y'know, that's what I thought at one time. When I first became a Christian, I read the Bible in two weeks. Then I didn't pick it up again for months. A while later, my youth leader encouraged me to start looking at the scriptures again, this time starting to read the Gospel stories, slowly and carefully. He told me to pray before I read, and to only read a small section at a time.

Andrew: Did you manage it?

John: More than that. It made me realise that when I'd sped through from Genesis to Revelation I'd got no more than a 'gist' of what it was about. When I started reading the portions of the Gospels in this new way something amazing happened. I got to see some of the 'truth' of what it was about. Sometimes I'd stay with just one passage for weeks. I'd read it again and again, chewing it over and trying to apply it to my life. It was then that I realised I had to live differently. It's like the words were soaking into me and beginning to change me.

Andrew: Really?

John: Yep. Do you see the difference now? The Bible is the living Word of God, so let it live in you.

Prayer

Prayer is an awesome gift to help you align yourself with God's will. Just like studying scripture, some people find it very easy and natural. Others find it more difficult. Again, there are loads of books and resources that might give you some useful pointers to help your prayer life, but one of the keys is to bear in mind that God is with us at all times, in all circumstances. It stands to reason then that we can communicate with him anytime, anyplace and about anything. If you're feeling inadequate because you don't spend an hour in quiet and con-templative prayer every morning and evening then cut yourself some slack. Instead, talk to God as though he were right next to you as you make your breakfast, walk to school, stand in line, meet with friends, play football, do your homework, get stood up by a friend(!)…When Paul encourages us to 'pray without ceasing', (1 Thessalonians 5:17), I doubt he meant for us to spend all our days on our knees before God.

Having said that of course, if we think of God as our friend who walks beside us all day, we also need to give him space to com-municate with us. Remember, prayer is not a one way conversa-tion. It's a time when we should expect to hear from God. That's why a regular discipline that allows you a little more space and time to commune with him can be very helpful. It still need not be

If prayer is a natural way of talking to God, why can it be so difficult?

Probably because prayer is so powerful. (The Bible, from the Old to the New Testament is full of stories that show us this.) When we realise the power of prayer we also recognise that the enemy of God will seek to destroy it. Read Ephesians 6 about the fight we're involved in and the importance of the armour of God. Notice how prayer is the most crucial part of the fight. Remember that it is sin that separates from God, which is why Jesus taught us to confess our sins as we come before God in prayer (Matt 6:12). When God deals with your sin he will move in power through your prayers.

the traditional picture of the child at prayer, kneeling at the bedside with his eyes shut and his hands clasped in some pious pose. How about, for example, taking a quiet walk alone; or sitting comfortably with the lights off and some relaxing or inspiring music. Some people like to light a candle and stare into its flame. Others like to meditate on a passage of scripture and use it as a prayer. Imagine God's delight, to have his own poetry read back to him in prayer and praise!

Some people find it helpful to practise 'fasting' to help with prayer. The idea is to skip a meal (or something you enjoy or feel you 'need') and let your hunger remind you how your soul hungers for Jesus. If you'd normally spend an hour eating lunch, or watching Eastenders and Coronation Street, commit to spending that time instead concentrating on communicating with God. If you think fasting is something that might help you, talk to someone you know who practises it, or pick up one of the many good books on the subject

PART 1: YOUR STORY ⊙

> I will pray out loud
> I will pray in my head
> I will pray with my eyes shut, or my eyes open,
> Sometimes with my head bowed,
> Sometimes with my hands up.
> I will pray about everything
> With a thankful heart
> With a broken heart
> Without ceasing.
> I will pray through scripture
> I might keep a journal
> I might pray in song
> I will pray in the spirit and in truth.
> I will pray during an exam
> Washing the dishes
> Cleaning my room
> I will pray in silence
> I will talk
> **I will listen.**

Don't let anything break your prayer connection.

Even if you're feeling far away from God stay with him in prayer. Remember, God reached down to you through Jesus. He knows you're not perfect and doesn't need you to be. So, no matter how badly you mess up, God stays connected to you. No matter how badly you express yourself or how random and desperate your communication is, your prayers fuel a powerful connection.

Thanksgiving

This might sound like an old-fashioned word, but it can be something that really alters our mood and shapes our outlook on life. It's easy to be cynical about things, to trust no-one, to only believe what we can see, touch and feel, to expect the worst from people and situations, to be critical. The easiest way to move away from all that is to keep a thankful heart. In his letter to the Thessalonians, Paul instructed them to 'give thanks whatever happens. That is what God wants for you in Christ Jesus' (1 Thessalonians 5:18). When we make a conscious effort to view our world and our circumstances in this way it can have phenomenal effect. So start by thanking God for what you have, instead of moaning about what you don't have. Life in Gratefulland is much better than a day trip to Disneyland! Your new attitude will not only directly benefit you, but, all of a sudden, you'll become a fascinating person to those around you. Think about it. If, even in difficult and stressful circumstances, you are seen with a positive attitude born out of a grateful heart and trust in God, you will inevitably have something your friends want to know about.

I am thankful
For who I am, and who I am not
For what I have, and what I have not
I am thankful that I have many things to give thanks for.
When my day goes wrong, I will still be thankful because
He gives me the choice to be that way.
I am thankful in all things and others are curious.

Obedience

Yep, here's a tough one. Sounds like we're in line for a whole load of rules and restrictions. The thing to remember is that in the long run being obedient to God ultimately makes life a whole lot easier for us. Think of the young child whose parents tell him never to touch the fireplace. He might fight, argue and find it wholly unfair to be given such a rule, but his parents know that one day the fireplace will be very hot and the child will be seriously hurt if he touches it. The rule is not given to spoil the child's fun, but to protect him. 'All very well', you might say, 'but how do I know what the rules are?' Well, aside from the Ten Commandments (see if you can name them all—if you can't, take a look at Exodus 20), our best example of obedience is Jesus himself. The more we know his story, the more we can allow him to shape ours. The other thing is just the way we are wired. Particularly as Christians we find ourselves intrinsically knowing when we're pushing the boundaries. This, again, is the Holy Spirit within us. He longs to protect us, to provide for us, to keep us safe. Obedience, then, is telling the truth, no matter what. It's protecting our affections; it's walking away from a situation that we're longing to dive into; or making ourselves stand when we'd rather run. Yes, it can be tough, but disobedience leaves us hiding from, not connecting with, God.

I will discover God when

I'm telling the truth and getting into trouble

When I'm leaving a bad party when it feels good

When I'm accepting the authority of parents and leaders.

I will meet God in obedience and discipline

And dance in his freedom.

Service

What do we mean by service? Well, I'd like to define it very simply as, 'helping other people'. It's as easy as that. Or is it? Well, yes, there are lots of good and helpful people around and, again, I suspect it's just something to do with the way we human beings are wired. It's natural (to most people anyway) to want to help others. But as followers of Christ we have a tough example to follow. Jesus himself was the ultimate servant, laying down his life for those he loved (irrespective of whether or not they loved him back).

PART 1: YOUR STORY ⊙

Hopefully we won't be called to do that, but still, we are given a fairly weighty challenge. In the book of Galatians we're actually instructed to serve one another 'with love' (Gal 5:13). Very quickly after that we're told exactly the enormity of that love: 'Love your neighbour as you love yourself' (Gal 5:14). I might also point out here that 'love' is a verb. It's a 'doing' word; a thing that involves continuous action. There's a challenge. But it is also said that in loving someone they can become lovely. Again, we'll need to rely on the Holy Spirit here, but as we ask God to help us love someone we struggle with, we will begin to see things that are lovely in them. We will begin to see them through Jesus' eyes, not just our own. Wow!

Perhaps this is really stirring you up to dedicate your life to the service of others through God's love within you. If so, that's great. However, it's perhaps more likely to have you feeling doubtful about your motivation and wondering how on earth you're supposed to apply this to your life as it is, without going off to work in the Salvation Army soup kitchens.

Acts of kindness get noticed.

When you make others feel good, you feel good and the light of Jesus shines through you. Read the book of Romans for lots of good teaching on how to live in service to others.

Let me just say, 'Don't worry.' Great things often start small and remember the good part: that everything you do out of an authentic heart of service is ultimately a service for God.

Take my friend Jude, for example. Every Thursday after school she calls by the local old people's home. There she sits and talks with an old lady who has no family to visit her. When Jude walks in the room the old lady's face lights up with joy. Jude sees Jesus. When she holds the old lady's hand and listens to her stories of days gone by she holds the hand of Jesus. As Jude says, 'I could spend that hour at the shopping mall or watching TV, but when I visit the home I spend it with Jesus'.

You may remember that Message 2000 (Initiated by Soul Survivor, Youth For Christ, The Message and Oasis Trust) made the people of Manchester sit up and take notice in this way. They 'served' the community, clearing rubbish, taking part in community projects, helping in schools and all manner of public services. Today's culture does not expect such acts of love and service and, consequently, their voluntary efforts raised many questions from curious onlookers. What a story!

When you're thinking about 'service', start by considering the small and everyday things. In all situations, think, 'what would Jesus do'. Perhaps he'd wash the dishes, clean a room, turn off the TV, read to a young child, visit a friend in need, cook a meal, carry some shopping, speak words of encouragement, give to charity, take out the rubbish, do a sponsored walk for charity…get the picture?

There are many tools to help us 'connect' and we've only got space to look at a few here. Take some time to think of other ways in which we might seek a glimpse or experience of God…through worship, nature, in silence, through suffering, fellowship with other believers, study, service…Some will be more natural to you than others. Try many, and bear in mind that what doesn't particularly excite you today might be the very same thing that finds you in close intimacy with God tomorrow. Also recognise that what works for you may not work for your friend. You might find God in a rock concert, she might seek him in the quiet places, on a walk alone, listening to his whispers in the trickling of a stream. This recognition that we are all wired slightly differently is important later on when we come to look at how we listen to our friend's stories and interweave them with our own.

So let's recap. We've recognised that we do not have to (and could not) earn our way into God's good books, because Jesus has already made that way for us. However, as we ask him to transform us, to help us grow more like Jesus, we understand that God has given us many tools—not least the Holy Spirit—to enable us to learn from him, to grow in him, to experience him and to love him.

The reason behind all this is because the authenticity of our relationship with God largely underpins 'three story evangelism', the very thing we're looking at here. Remember, three story living relies on relationships and if our relationships are weak or phoney, it's simply not going to work.

Three story living is as much about you as it is about them. Remember earlier I said that the more God does in you, the more he can do through you? This was a lesson that those closest to Jesus had to learn. Let's look at Luke 5 and the report of Jesus calling his first followers. A quick glance at the passage might leave us believing that Simon (later to be called Peter) 'left everything and followed Jesus', because of the miracle of the large catch of fish. Simon and his colleagues had been out fishing all night and caught nothing. As commercial fishermen this would be a big problem. Their livelihood was at stake. Jesus joined them and suddenly their nets were full. Certainly, many people come to Jesus when they realise he can meet their need. We'll be looking at this a bit more later. But let's look at what really happened here. In actual fact, the depth of the story has more to do with what was beginning to happen in Simon's life. In chapter 4 we are told that Jesus had visited Simon's house and healed his mother-in-law. So Simon had seen enough to be very curious about Jesus and to know that there was something very special about him. But imagine the scene when Jesus instigates a fishing trip in the middle of the day. To do as Jesus asked—take the boat into deep water and cast the nets—went against everything Simon knew. He had been out all night and caught nothing, and everyone knows you don't go fishing in the daytime! He said as much to Jesus, but something was obviously stirring within him and he said, 'But you say to put the nets in the water, so I will.' This is an act of obedience to Jesus. It made no sense to Simon, but there was something that made him take the risk of looking foolish in front of his friends and do as he was told. Of course, you know the story. The nets became so full of fish that they began to break and suddenly the water was a frenzy of fishermen trying to fill the boats and at the same time save them from sinking with the load. But what's going on with Peter at this time? He's not involved with the frenzy. No, something much more profound and exciting is happening to him. 'He bowed down before Jesus and said, "Go away from me, Lord. I am a sinful man!"' Do you get what's happening? Simon has recognised Jesus as someone whose very being exposes sin. Jesus had said nothing about sin, but in his presence—the presence of God—Simon has become profoundly aware of his sinfulness. The atmosphere must have been electric. And what does

Jesus do? 'Don't be afraid. From now on you will fish for people,' he tells Simon. It's as though Jesus is saying, 'Now that you've realised what you are, and a little of who I am to you, we can begin our journey. And it's going to be a big one. We're going to be doing some really great things and many more are going to be joining us because of what we can do together.'

Simon Peter's journey began with a response to something he knew he couldn't ignore. He didn't suddenly know everything about Jesus and I'm sure that, as a humble fisherman, he could never imagine having an impact in God's cosmic story. But he did. We watch some of his journey unfold in the Gospel stories and the letters that follow. It turns out that he did actually 'go out to all the world', but note that prior to this he was to simply walk along with Jesus, so he could really begin to know him. Like the other apostles, he spent time living alongside Jesus, learning from him, watching, listening, learning to be like him. Even before the Holy Spirit was given in that dramatic account in Acts, God was working through Peter, because he was very much working in him.

So, it's time for some self-assessment, an MOT, if you like, before we continue the journey. We're not looking to become Mr or Miss perfect Christian. There is no such thing this side of heaven. But if you are doubtful of your relationship with Jesus, it's time to put a few things straight, to check out your own connection to God's story, before you try connecting others.

Take, for example, the salesman who sells electronic personal organisers. He takes the job because it seems like a good idea at the time. The product sounds okay and he needs the money. He knows he's a good salesman. In fact his friends say he could sell ice to Eskimos. He's got all the talk, all the bravado and he knows how to close a deal. In fact, he's so confident in his own ability that he doesn't bother to get to know how the organisers work properly. He knows the basics about what they should do, but he doesn't take time to sit and study the handbook or any of the function keys and he can't really be bothered putting in his personal details and diary. After a few weeks, the salesman is called into the office to see his boss. It turns out he is way off meeting his target and there have been complaints from customers about his timekeeping and the fact that he misses appointments or double books others. 'The problem', says his boss, 'is that you obviously don't know the product. You may know a little bit about it, but you don't believe in it enough to use it yourself. You try to keep your schedule in your head, rather than letting the organiser help you and our potential customers see you struggling with the very same problems they have. Any wonder then they don't buy into the product you're trying to sell. What kind of advertisement do you think you are?!'

TALK BACK

Sharon: *I've been reading some of this stuff about how it's important to connect with God before I try to connect others to him, and I'm pretty sure I get it, but I'm really worried about where it leaves me.*

John: *In what sense?*

Sharon: *Well, I think I've always had a connection with God. My parents have brought me up as a Christian and I know God exists, the same way as I know the wind blows or the sun shines. I've always talked to him and never had cause to doubt him, but when I look at some of my Christian friends I think I'm missing something.*

John: *What is it you think you're missing Sharon?*

Sharon: *That's just it, I don't know. But, take Darren. He's only been a Christian for a month but he talks about Jesus all the time. He stands up with his arms outstretched during worship sessions and always prays out loud in church. The other big thing is he speaks in tongues. I've never done that. I worry that it's because I might not really be a Christian after all. When we first met, Darren asked me how long I'd been a Christian and I said 'always'. He gave me a funny look and said I probably hadn't made a proper commitment. He told me what had happened to him, how he was at a Christian concert and went forward to the front when the lead singer asked if there was anyone who wanted to give their life to Jesus. He said he was just bursting with excitement. It sounded so cool. I've never had an experience like that.*

John: Do you love Jesus Sharon?

Sharon: Yes, of course.

John: What makes you say that.

Sharon: I just do. I know I do, because I do. See what I mean? It sounds like a pathetic answer, but it's true, so that's all I can say. It's hardly going to convince anyone else is it?

John: Sharon, I've known you for long enough now to be sure that you walk with Jesus. You mentioned about speaking in tongues. That's a very precious gift of the Spirit, as we read in 1 Corinthians 12, but you should not forget what it means to have the 'fruits' of the Spirit. Read Galatians 5: 22. I'd say you're a pretty good example of love, joy, peace, patience, kindness, goodness, gentleness, self-control, faithfulness…See what I'm saying? You should be encouraged. And I know that over the years lots of new people have joined the youth group because of their friendship with you—probably more a case of who you are than whether or not you lift your hands in worship and appear to be super spiritual.

Sharon: Thanks John. That means a lot. But what about this 'conversion' experience you hear people talk about. I'm still not sure I've had one. In fact, sometimes I try to create one by making myself commit to God again and again. I try in my mind to go through the steps. Y'know tell myself I know I'm a sinner, say sorry to God, ask him to come into my life. But I never get that warm fuzzy feeling you hear some people talk about when they do that.

John: Well, there's nothing wrong with that. Actually, if we started each day asking God to forgive us our wrongdoings and walk with us through the day, we'd be much better off. But let's put warm and fuzzies aside for a while and take a look at the disciple Peter and his 'conversion experience', as you call it. When do you think it was?

PART 1: YOUR STORY ⊙

Sharon: Well, there's that really famous passage when he declares that Jesus is the son of God after Jesus has asked the disciples who they think he is.

John: Yes, you're talking about Matthew 16 verse 16. But what about earlier when the disciples first met Jesus in the fishing boat. There, in Luke 5, we're told how Peter left his nets and followed Jesus. I'd say that's a pretty big commitment, wouldn't you.

Sharon: Oh, yeah. Was that it then do you think?

John: Could be, but what about in John 1:42 when Jesus changes his name from Simon to Peter; or Matthew 14:33 when Peter declares 'truly you are the Son of God', just after he walked on the water with Jesus; or was it as he saw Jesus after his resurrection when he fed his followers on the beach, as recorded in John 21. Then again, what does it mean in Acts 2 when the Holy Spirit comes and Peter suddenly has this supernatural gift and authority. I bet that was a pretty 'warm and fuzzy' experience, eh?

Sharon: Yeah, I see what you're saying. Peter made a lot of declarations and commitments.

John: The other thing Sharon, is the truly human side of Peter. He was a wonderful disciple in so many ways and God used him powerfully, but don't forget there were many times when he really messed up and let Jesus down. Go back to his big confession in Matthew 16. It's not long after that when we see Peter asking some really dumb questions of Jesus and making some big mistakes. Remember, for all his big announcements and commitments, he actually denied even knowing Jesus when the pressure was really on!

Sharon: I never even thought of that.

John: Jesus loved Peter and he knew him really well. Remember, he even predicted that Peter would deny knowing him when the pressure was on. He knew he *would mess up, but Jesus also knew that in his heart of hearts, Peter was really committed to him. He also knows you the same way. Be encouraged. Continue to commit yourself to him every day. Perhaps one day you'll be given one of those supernatural gifts, but for now, remain faithful and sure of him. We should always be looking to develop our relationship with God, so focus on that. I know that you're very good at serving others and I have a feeling you find God when you're alone and quiet. So maybe now try some different tools to help you move on in your journey with him.*

Sharon: *Yes. That really helps. I guess I need to stop doubting myself so much and just stay focussed on what I know deep down.*

PART 1: YOUR STORY ⟩

Okay, just one more thing then, before we move on. We all have times when we feel far away from God, perhaps when our walk with Jesus has become more ritual than reality and we've wandered off the track. Sadly, this is a natural and common thing and—though it's important to recognise that fact so that we don't beat ourselves up about it too much—it is a sure sign that we need to take action quickly. Remember, the thing that separates us from God in the first place is sin. Thankfully, because of Jesus and that thing called 'grace', we do not have to remain in that separation.

Don't expect to be able to interest others in God if you don't have a good relationship with him.

First make sure you've said sorry to him for the things you've done that have let him down. Secondly make sure you don't continue to do those things and ask God to help you.

However, God's grace is not an easy 'get-out clause' that allows us to continue in sin. So at times when we're feeling distant from God we should take an important review. Am I behaving in a way that is displeasing to God?

(Have I gossiped, lied, stolen, got drunk, disobeyed, pushed sexual boundaries, cheated…) Also ask, have I been 'connecting' to God in a meaningful way?

When we ponder these questions we can begin to come up with a course of action. We can confess, ask forgiveness for sin and ensure we do not put ourselves in a position of temptation to continue down that path. We can look at the way we have been using the tools we have to 'connect' (worship, Bible reading, prayer, thanksgiving, service etc.). We can tell a trusted friend so they can help us through the difficulty and, above all, we should ask God on a daily basis to help us grow closer to him and make space to hear his voice.

Above all, persevere with your desire to get to know him better. There's that famous passage in Revelation 3:20 when God says, 'Here I am! I stand at the door and knock. If you hear my voice and open the door, I will come in and eat with you, and you will eat with me.' Think of it that way. God keeps calling at your house, all you have to do is invite him in. If you don't do that he won't force his way in. He'll just wait until you're ready to answer the door, but until you do you'll be missing out on the great time you could have sharing a meal together.

All friendships and relationships require effort by both parties. Okay, so we do have the added hurdle of not being able to 'communicate' with God in the physical. But the Bible tells us, 'Let the peace that Christ gives control your thinking' (Col. 3:15). Have you ever thought that what you might call your 'conscience' is actually God communicating with you? If we are living in a way that is displeasing to God, his peace leaves us and we have inner turmoil. That's when we know that we're going against God's will. Take a good look at what Jesus said about vines and branches in John chapter 15. In verse 5 Jesus says, 'I am the vine, and you are the branches. If any remain in me and I remain in them, they produce much fruit. But without me they can do nothing.' In verse 7 he goes on, 'If you remain in me and follow my teachings, you can ask anything you want, and it will be given to you. You should produce much fruit and show that you are my followers, which brings glory to my Father.'

TALK BACK

John: You're really struggling with all this aren't you Simon?

Simon: Trouble is, I do feel distant from God right now. In fact, for months I haven't been able to pray properly, I don't want to go to church and I haven't even opened my Bible. There's so much other rubbish going on in my life and God just doesn't seem relevant any more. And none of it's my fault. I don't think it's me who's sinning!

John: Talk to me about this other rubbish.

Simon: Well, yesterday topped it all. I got another fail mark for my latest maths assignment, which probably means I'm going to blow my chances of being able to do the physics 'A' Level.

John: I thought you were good at maths?

Simon: I'm supposed to be, but I'm not getting a chance to do any of the work properly. I'm living over the other side of town now with Mum and it takes me nearly an hour to get home. Then, when I get there, the house is so noisy with the younger kids, and I don't have my own room any more to work in. I'd go back to Dad's, but he's so tied up with his new lady friend that I feel like I'm not wanted there.

John: You're going through a really difficult time, in all sorts of ways, aren't you? We need to talk more, and have a look at some practical things to help you out. The world has a nasty habit of throwing this kind of stuff at you. No-one promised life would be easy or even pleasant, but I know it's really rough when you feel you're being let down by people time after time.

Simon: Yeah, it's just not fair! None of this is my fault. Has God abandoned me or something? Why is he letting this happen? Why me?

> *John:* You know, we have lots of promises in the Bible and, at times like this, it can be a good idea to take a close look at them. It might help if you write them out or even try to pray them back to God. The Apostle John tells us that, as a child of God, we have 'victory that conquers the world'. Read 1 John 5:1–15 and Romans 8:31–39. I'm not saying it will solve your problems, but it will help lift your spirit just now and give you hope and encouragement to stay close to God. It's not nice, but some people find that suffering itself can lead to a very precious connection with God. Remember, too, the story about the footprints in the sand.
>
> *Simon:* What's that?
>
> *John:* Looking back over his life, a man saw two sets of footprints in the sand as he walked side by side with Jesus. Then, when he looked closer, he saw that during difficult times of wilderness there was only one set of footprints. When he asked Jesus why he had abandoned him during these times, Jesus pointed out that it was then that he had picked him up and carried him.

So here we are at the end of the beginning. We've acknowledged that sharing Jesus is more about 'coming' than 'going'; and probably more about 'us' than 'them'. Bearing that in mind, I hope you're now more interested in exploring how three story living can really begin to connect our friends' stories to God as they get to know our story. Our journey with God is made through lots of different pathways and we're all on slightly different routes at different times. The key is to make sure we find our place on the map, to ensure we stay connected, for our own sake, and for the sake of those we're going to talk about next…

PART 2: THEIR STORY
CHAPTER 3: **LISTEN DON'T LEAP**

Have you ever stopped to think about how many people you know? Consider how many people you communicate with on a weekly basis—family members, friends of your family who visit your home, classmates, people you see regularly on the bus or through clubs and interest groups you might be a part of. Chances are, you communicate with more people now than you will at any other time of your life. As we get older, our circles of contact tend to get smaller as we have more choice about the people we spend time with. From our first day at school, we're thrown together with a large bunch of people. Some become friends, others are no more than 'classmates', but chances are we at least have some basic communication with them on a regular basis. In our mid and late teens, our circles of communication expand even more as we find ourselves with people from other forms or classes for certain subjects. Later, we might find ourselves dropped into a completely new arena as we go to a different college. Think back over the last five years and consider the different groups you have been part of, either by choice or by given circumstance. Then consider that of your parents. It's probable that they have had the same job, the same bunch of friends and, by and large, the same social routines for as long as you can remember.

What's the point here? Well, let's go back to our stories again. Remember, every individual has their own story. If we consider the number of stories that interweave, even in a small way, with our own, we soon recognise the potential number that can also be interwoven with God's story. Excited? You should be. Intimidated? You might be. See, we need to blow out of the water any idea you may still have about evangelism being something we go and 'do' to people far away. Yes, in Matthew 28, Jesus instructed us to go and make followers of all people in the world, but he never said 'don't bother with those closest to you'! He also said lots of other things that add weight to the basis of our three story living idea: that it is through 'relationships' that we most effectively communicate the Gospel. Romans 15:13 says, 'I pray that the God who gives hope will fill you with much joy and peace while you trust in him. Then your hope will overflow by the power of the Holy Spirit.' Now do you see why everything we talked about in chapter 2 is so important? If we are living in the peace and joy of Christ, the hope and trust we have in him will simply overflow and be witnessed and experienced by all who interact with us. All this, without us even saying a word!

So, now we've established that there are already loads of stories that are intertwined in our own, let's take a look at how we can really begin to develop relationships in a way that will ultimately lead them into God's story. Prepare yourself, it might be that there are a few surprises in store, even among your closest friends.

Building relationships is not usually something we consciously think about. We just do it. It would be very strange if, when we were introduced to someone, we sat down and told them our life story. For one thing, we wouldn't have the time. For another, why should we? Usually, before we reveal things about ourselves we need to gain the other person's trust. Unless we're seeing this person for some kind of therapy, we also like to see that they are interested enough in us to reveal something of themselves.

In the Old Testament, Job asked the question, 'Can you understand the secrets of God?' The answer, of course, is 'No'. 1 Corinthians 13:12 says, 'Now we see a dim reflection, as if we were looking into a mirror, but then we shall see clearly. Now I know only a part, but then I will know fully, as God has known me.' The reason we do not see God clearly is more to do with us than him. God has revealed his full story to us through Christ. He has chosen to make himself vulnerable, chosen to make himself open, accessible and fully committed to us. That's probably what Jesus meant in John 14 when he said that if you want to know what God is like, look at me. As we continue on our journey with God we begin to see more clearly that which is there for us. In a similar sense, that's the way all relationships work. Our friends don't reveal their full story when we first meet them, but it is in this process of revealing ourselves to each other over time that a strong and trusting relationship is developed. By revealing more of ourselves we grow the relationship and, in turn, our friends reveal more of who they really are. If a person does not want to reveal anything of themselves, there is very little we can do. We cannot force them into a relationship with us, however this is where our love for them—lead by the Holy Spirit—will keep us patient and committed. As Jesus stands at the door and knocks until we answer, so with other people, we should wait patiently and gently build a friendship based on listening, on being there, on being relaxed with no agenda or pressure. What we're talking about here is not a 'technique'. We're talking about love, and a desire to tell the greatest story ever told, simply because we know how much God loves us.

Listening and revealing is what lies at the heart of three story living. To become accomplished in the art of connection, it's important to practise the art of listening, so that we might be invited to reveal. **Let's drop in at John's place...**

TALK BACK

Greg: I don't know what the problem is with Nick. He doesn't seem to want to hang out this week.

John: I thought you two had become good friends?

Greg: I thought so too, but I'm not going to bother any more, he's just so miserable. It's not like I haven't tried. Last Saturday he texted me to say that he'd come round, so I got Sarah and Luke and a couple of others from my karate club together and we watched a video at my house. It was a good night.

John: *What did you talk about?*

Greg: *Well, we didn't. We just watched the film. Anyway, I saw Nick on Sunday at football and we got together for a burger afterwards. Now I come to think of it, he seemed quiet then. I was telling him about Lisa, this girl I'm going to ask out. I suppose I did go on a bit, but she's so cool, and I think she likes me too. At least that's what Maria, her friend, said to me...*

John: *What did Nick say?*

Greg: *Well, not a lot really, like I said, he was pretty quiet. I wonder if he's jealous. He's not been in touch since. I bet it's cos he's not been out with a girl...*

John: *It might be something else.*

Greg: *Like what?*

John: *Well, you won't know until you listen to him, will you?*

Greg: *I can't be bothered with him if he's just going to be jealous.*

John: *Be careful of making assumptions like that, Greg. Actually Nick came to see me last night. He's feeling really lonely right now. I'm not going to tell you his problems, but he does have a big one at the moment. He really needs a friend to listen to him.*

Greg: *Oh...well, why didn't he just say?*

John: *It sounds to me like he tried, but this is a very upsetting thing and he wouldn't just come out with it in the middle of watching a video with a bunch of people he hardly knows.*

Greg: *And Sunday...well, yes, I suppose I just went on about Lisa...so what now?*

John: How about giving him a call. Grab a coke together. Above all, Greg, try to keep your mouth shut more and your ears open. Get what I'm saying?

Greg: Hearing you loud and clear boss!

Jesus was a master at listening and revealing and he did it purely out of genuine interest in a person. When he met with an individual he, being God, already knew their needs, but he often asked questions and engaged them in conversation anyway. This was because he loved them. He was genuinely interested in them and he wanted them to feel this so they would be able to reveal things about themselves, to themselves. Think of a few incidents where Jesus met people. Read, for example, about the Samaritan woman at the well (John 4). Notice how Jesus very often asked leading questions (some of them very puzzling) before he healed a person, taught them or met their need in some other way. Questions can play a very important part in the art of listening. They show a person you are interested. They can also help a person formulate what they really think because they have to approach what they're communicating through your question.

Remember in chapter two we touched on the idea that people come to Jesus because of 'need'? One of the big things about three story living is establishing the 'need' of those we talk to. Questions can be the key. Questions allow people to go places within themselves that they probably would not otherwise go. A listener, asking relevant questions at the right time and in the right way, can often open up emotions, fears and points of pain that may have been deeply buried and would certainly not have been volunteered.

The Art of listening:

Don't butt in. Don't rehearse what you're going to say. Don't judge. Don't try to offer pat solutions to problems. Don't hijack the conversation with your own agenda. Show you're interested by making good eye contact. Ask questions related to what you're being told. Keep confidences, so that a trust is built between you.

Listening

I need to listen to people, to really listen,
To stay out of the way of their thoughts,
To be a safe place for them to share their fears,
Hopes,
Frustrations,
Brokenness,
Anger,
Dreams,
Desires,
Embarrassments,
Loneliness,
Confusion.
I will listen to their story no matter how long it takes
No matter what is said
No matter where it takes us.
I will be caring
Humble
Compassionate
Open
Understanding
Fun.
I will be a friend.

A good listener will ultimately be invited to speak. That is, if you spend time taking notice of a person, listening to him, showing interest in him, caring for him and gently loving him, there will come a time when he will want to know what really makes you tick. So remember, unless we listen, we don't really earn the right to speak. Unless we can listen to their story we cannot begin to reveal ours in any depth and we will not be invited to tell God's story.

Conversation between friends is relaxed and very naturally made up of questions and debates. In this environment there is no pressure. This is very important in three story living. If the relationship is right, you should not feel anxious about getting your message across, about forcing understanding or about pushing for a response. Think about a close friend and how you got to know him or her. You were once strangers. Then, you became friends as you talked, listened to one another, shared experiences, realised mutual interests, spent time together. You may not have realised it at the time, but the friendship would have developed as you revealed things about yourself that only those close to you would know. That doesn't necessarily mean you shared secrets, but it does mean they know more about who you are and what makes you tick, rather than just basic information, like the subjects you study at school and what mobile tariff you're on. In this environment you should find yourself naturally being able to introduce God's story as you share your own. And you will have begun to do this because you will have been given the invitation. Your story will provoke questions in your friend that you can respond to in a relaxed and natural way.

You will also find that, as you get to know a person well, you will be able to tell your story in the light of what you understand in theirs. Think about it, a person's story will inevitably shape the way they interpret yours. We'll be looking at this in a little more depth later.

Ready for the bad news?

All this openness and 'revealing' leaves you vulnerable. You see, that's the big thing about the kind of relationships we're talking about here. Don't be fooled into thinking that as the Christian you have to be all-knowing and have life sussed. Don't think that you have to be able to present a picture of a totally transformed life. Remember, if Christianity is a journey, we are still very much trying to find our place on the map. Those who appear to have reached the destination and come back to collect others are phoney at best and sickening at worst. No, as we discussed in the first part of this book, to be taken seriously we need to be authentic, we need to be honest, we can only be ourselves, zits and all!

Certainly, there is good news. It is likely to be our vulnerability that opens up the story for our friends. If you tell your story, including your fears, dreams, disappointments and delusions, your friend will be able to comfortably reveal deeper parts of themselves to you. But let's not get too hung up about this. If you're not finding yourself with a comfortable and natural opportunity to tell God's story, you will still have developed a friendship.

Let's remember that friendships usually continue to develop and, somewhere down the road, who knows what you're going to explore together? So be yourself. Be honest, be vulnerable and don't worry about an agenda. Don't feel pressured into introducing God's story until you're invited, or you're sure the timing is absolutely right through a Holy Spirit moment.

Yes, it's time to get naked (not literally!). The more you reveal, the more freedom there will be to share with each other and the more you will understand your friend's potential recognition point for their need of Jesus.

TALK BACK

Chris: *I've been reading this stuff and it all sounds a bit 'hippy man, yeah chill out and get naked with one another'! It's like some kind of therapy. I never thought about how I make friends before, I just do it. And all that listening stuff…oh boy, I'm scared to say anything now!*

John: *Okay, chill out. You really don't need to get tied up with it all. What do you talk about with your friends?*

Chris: *Dunno. Just stuff. Music, computer games, girls…usual thing.*

John: *What about when your Dad went into hospital last year and all the worry about the cancer. Didn't you talk to your mates about that?*

Chris: *Well, yeah, some of the others knew about it. Nick, Emma, Sarah, Andy. In fact, I suppose I really talked to Andy. He knew what it was like because of when his mum died. He even came to the hospital with me quite a few times and he really helped when there were times I couldn't stop crying.*

John: *So you opened up to him, just as he must have opened up to you.*

Chris: *I suppose you're right. Okay, then help me with this one. There's this new group I've been going around with* now I've joined the football club. They're a great laugh but last week we got onto talking about God and stuff.

John: Oh yeah? That's great.

Chris: Well yes, I suppose it was. It all started 'cos they wanted to know why I couldn't come training on a Wednesday evening and I told them it was because of the group. So they wanted to know all about it. What we talked about, who we were, all that sort of stuff.

John: So you told them.

Chris: Yes. I suppose they could have just taken the 'mick' out of me being 'God Squad', but actually they were really interested. Trouble is, they just bombarded me with questions. I couldn't get my head together to think straight about what I was saying.

John: In those situations you need to try to slow things down. Instead of panicking about how to give your answers, try asking a question back. Make yourself some space and get them thinking, rather than just asking.

Chris: Easier said than done!

John: Yes, but you had a great opener there. You've not known these people long, but they obviously like you, and you've revealed something really important about yourself that hasn't put them off. Things will grow from here, and I bet it's not long before you're having some really great chats with a few of them. So for now, be patient. Pray for them, of course. And the other thing Chris, they'll be taking notice of how you operate. Remember when we were studying Matthew 5, about being salt and light in the world? How you behave and the things you say are extra important now. Look up Ephesians 4:29–32. 'When you talk, do not say harmful things, but say what people need—words that will help others become stronger…and verse 32, 'Be kind and loving to each other, and forgive each other just as God forgave you in Christ.' Memorise

> these kinds of passages and let them be your checkpoint. This will be the best way to make opportunities to really communicate your story…
>
> **Chris:** No pressure then!
>
> **John:** Well, you see what I'm saying, but don't stress out about it. Even if you blow it, the story will still be out there and you're not on your own, are you.

This idea of 'timing' is very important in three story living. Imagine if the first time you visited someone's house you helped yourself to the contents of the fridge, launched yourself feet first onto the sofa and took over the TV control. You will have broken boundaries and intruded into personal space, most likely leaving your host shocked and offended. Do you see what I'm getting at? Don't push or pressure. Don't make assumptions. If you do, you'll be acting out of your own agenda, not God's (that's not to say God can't retrieve the situation, but it would be better if you didn't jump in and cause the offence in the first place). Remember, the timing is not your own. As Christians we have the Holy Spirit living within us. He is our guide and our helper. So trust his timing. After all, don't imagine that when you find yourself able to tell your story, it is of your own engineering. This should bring comfort and encouragement. You are not alone. Remember that God knows the heart of your hearer long before and in far more detail than you do. Your job is to present your story in the light of God's love and to present God's story in the only way you can. That is, authentically, through your own story, in his timing.

St Francis of Assisi said, 'Preach the Gospel at all times and when necessary use words.' That's worth thinking about. Remember, we're looking at three story 'living', not three story 'talking'. So, although there will come a time when you really want to verbalise things, much of God's story can be communicated through you simply by your actions, by your life. Jesus was, and is, God's story, the Gospel. He 'lived' and 'loved' the Gospel with every person he met. Depending on the person, he connected to them in a very individual way. He touched the man suffering with leprosy, he wept with his friends at a funeral, he took a drink from the Samaritan woman. All were powerful communications, irrespective of any words spoken. Mother Teresa caught the attention of the whole world. Was it because she 'spoke' or 'preached' about poverty? No, many have done that and gone uncelebrated. Mother Teresa picked up dying bodies from the gutter and she loved them. A thousand sermons could not have communicated the love of God more strongly. Think about the kind of statement you can make through your actions. How about the guy being bullied at school. The one who no-one wants much to do with because he's not cool, he's not one of the crowd and it's easier to be like everyone else and stay away from him. What if you decide to stand with him? What if you take time to show him you care, not out of some sense of pity, but because you've asked Jesus to help you see this guy through his eyes? What message will that send to onlookers, especially if you're considered one of the cool crowd? It's a powerful thing to do. In reality, it's a brave thing to do, but it's absolutely what Jesus would have done; and what he can do through you now.

Jesus also knew that every encounter he had with a person could be left in God's hands. See, we're back to talking about timing again. Take encouragement knowing that the journeys you travel in your relationships all follow a well worn path. Jesus himself, not to mention Paul, Peter and many of the other first believers we know about, practised 'three story' living. It follows, therefore, that we can learn from their wisdom. Yes, it's time to visit the Bible again. **Let's consider Jesus' own teaching in Matthew 5: 13–15.**

> You are the salt of the earth. But if the salt loses its salty taste, it cannot be made salty again. It is good for nothing, except to be thrown out and walked on. You are the light that gives light to the world. A city that is built on a hill cannot be hidden. And people don't hide a light under a bowl. They put it on a lampstand so the light shines for all the people in the house. In the same way, you should be a light for other people. Live so that they will see the good things you do and will praise your Father in heaven.

Let's put this another way. It's like Jesus is saying, 'Let me tell you why you are here. You are here to be salt-seasoning that brings out the God-flavours of this earth. If you lose your saltiness, how will people taste God. You'll have lost your usefulness and end up being thrown in the bin. Here's another way to put it. You're here to be light, shining God's light into the dark places and bringing out the God-colours in the world. God is not a secret to be kept. We want to shout about him from the hilltops, where we can be most seen. If I give you my light, I don't expect you to hide. No, I want you on a lampstand so you can light up the world for all who see you.'

For further study, check out the Sermon on the Mount in Matthew 5, or indeed, read carefully Matthew chapters 5–7 where we find Jesus teaching about lifestyle. Notice that nowhere here does Jesus tell his listeners to go preach. Rather, he teaches them how to live so that their lives would be examples of people who love God. While there were some, the apostles, who he clearly did send out to preach (as today), he encouraged all his followers to live out the kingdom of God in their life.

Let's now look at a passage in 1 Peter 3:15

> But respect Christ as the holy Lord in your hearts. Always be
> ready to answer everyone who asks you to explain about the
> hope you have, but answer in a gentle way and with respect.

This passage barely needs explanation and every word in it is important. The first thing we are to do is live with Christ as our Lord. He should rule our lives. He should be our boss and our helper. When he is, something begins to happen. We have hope, even in the middle of struggle, pain and difficulty. Notice that Peter's scenario is then that people come to us to ask questions. That's because, as we've said over and over again, relationships are built on them asking and us answering and communicating God's story through our lives. Notice also that Peter says we must do this in a gentle way and with respect. We must not approach them with the attitude of having all the answers. We must not be pushy or proud, but gentle. 'Respect' is also a very important thing. Do not look down on a person because they are not a Christian, but respect them for who and what they are.

The Apostle Paul was also very clear in Colossians 4:4-6.

> Pray that I can speak in a way that will make it clear, as I
> should. Be wise in the way you act with people who are not
> believers, making the most of every opportunity. When you
> talk, you should always be kind and pleasant so you will be
> able to answer everyone in the way you should.

Paul wanted believers to pray that he would preach the message clearly.
Notice that He is talking very much about himself when he focuses on
preaching. To the Colossians he stresses that they watch the way they live.
He tells them to be wise in their relationships and their conversations. Just
like Peter and Jesus before him, Paul teaches that a life filled with God will
create thirst in others to know about Jesus.

TALK BACK

Maria: I hate coming to you with this stuff John, but I'm
really worried about Sue and some of the things that are
happening with the girls in our form.

John: We need to be careful not to gossip Maria, but if you
have genuine concerns you need to bring them to me, or
to another leader in the church. What's the problem?

Maria: Well, you know Sue is a fairly new Christian and,
being Sue, she's very outright and confident and not
afraid to talk about it.

John: Yes, she can be quite a character!

Maria: Well she's been talking a lot to our non-Christian
friends, which is more brave than I am, but I'm worried
about the impression they're getting.

John: Why, what do you mean?

Maria: Well, for all the talking, we all know that she's still
sleeping with her boyfriend, smoking, skipping school

sometimes and lying to her mum about where she goes every night. Her language can be really rough, in fact I don't think she even knows what she's saying sometimes!

John: You've got to understand, Sue has a pretty tough life and even when people meet Jesus, few or them are radically changed over night. I know that Sue has made a very real commitment to Jesus. She's at the beginning of her journey. We must pray for her and support her as she continues on that path and allows Jesus to transform her. Jesus said that all should come to him as little children. Think of Sue in this way. In fact, think of yourself in this way too. Like all of us, Sue has lots to learn, lots to discover. There will be many times when she gets it wrong. In fact, to you or anyone else watching, things could seem to get very messy. Remember, a child learning to walk falls over many times. But you can be sure that God is working in her, he's dealing with the mess and loving her all the more.

Maria: So how can I help?

John: Continue to pray and be there as a friend. She's known you a long time and she will notice the way you behave. You should also concentrate on your friendship with the other girls. Remember, they never asked to be preached at. Just be yourself and let them see Jesus in you. When the time is right they'll ask you questions and you'll find yourself sharing something of the hope you have and just what it is that makes you tick.

Now, let's recap on the important stuff. Three story living is about relationships, not teaching. Remember, no-one is looking for an evangelist, but most people are looking for a friend. It's about listening, not preaching; asking questions more than giving answers; sharing not dictating. It's about honesty, not perfection and more about what you do than what you say. It's about God's timing, not our own agendas and definitely more about life than about words.

PART 2: THEIR STORY

CHAPTER 4: **THE NEEDS OF A STORYMAKER**

So how are we getting on? Hopefully by now you're beginning to feel a little less intimidated by the whole idea of sharing Jesus. Perhaps you've already had opportunity to put what we've discovered into practice. Maybe you're still mulling over the things we covered in the first couple of chapters and are working on getting your own story back on track. If so, that's great. Remember, stories continue to develop and people drop in and out of them all the time. Relationships are not tidy. Because people and circumstances are forever evolving. We might say life is an art. At least, it's certainly not a formula. There are many paths and your route will never be the same as anyone else's. Yes, God is more of an artist than a theologian. He's a painter and a poet and his canvass and story book are as bright and beautiful and magnificent as creation itself. Within it, he paints us and breathes poetry and song into our mouths.

Sorry if we're getting a little too 'arty' here, but the picture I'm excited to paint is one of 'freedom': the fact that there is no one or 'right' way to communicate the Gospel. Everyone comes to Jesus in different ways and for different reasons. In fact, that's one of the key things we're going to focus on next.

So, we've discovered that the most important thing in three story living is to know God's story (in fact this might be better re-phrased, 'to live God's story'). As we focus on doing this it will naturally mean that our behaviour and outlook on life becomes attractive to our friends and they will begin to want to know our story and to share theirs. In the course of that happening, it is our hope that our friends will become curious about God's story and begin to want to connect it with their own. Sounds simple when put like that, but remember, three story living is not a 'technique', it's real, ragged, gritty, ever-changing life.

I mentioned earlier about everyone coming to Jesus in different ways. Whether we realise it or not, most people come to Jesus when they recognise he can satisfy their 'need'. Therefore, discerning our friend's point of need can be important in helping us sense how we might, when the time is right, introduce God's story. It's also important to recognise that what first brought us to Jesus is not necessarily the same thing that will bring our friend.

PART 2: THEIR STORY

TALK BACK

Jane: I was really surprised the other day when Karen asked me what made me want to become a Christian. I thought she was a Christian too?

John: As far as I know, she is. Think again about what she asked you.

Jane: What do you mean?

John: Well, my friend Mike told me how he got caught out with this one in his early days as a preacher and evangelist. When he made a response to Jesus it was because he realised God's promise of being a loving Father. This was a very special thing for Mike. He had a fantastic dad, so to think of God in this way, as one who loved him with such strength, was right on his wavelength. He also knew all the wonderful and positive things about 'love'. He was surrounded by it. He had a great family and a secure community of friends. When he started preaching he would focus heavily on this very precious message of the loving father. He came unstuck when he met Sandra.

Jane: What was the problem?

John: Well, Sandra attended one of his meetings and Mike realised afterwards that she seemed very irritated. It took quite some time to find out what the problem was. In fact, Mike ended up counselling her over several weeks. It turned out she hated her father. Though he often told her he loved her, he abused her. For Sandra, 'love' was so mixed up with abuse that her understanding of a father – child relationship was a million miles away from that of Mike's.

Jane: He was lucky she stayed in the meeting at all!

John: Exactly. It taught Mike a huge lesson in making assumptions about communicating Jesus.

People are complex and complicated. Whilst it's been said that you can identify certain personality types and behaviour traits, we are very much individuals. Psalm 139 celebrates this and gives praise to the God who made us 'in an amazing and wonderful way.' People cannot be labelled. They don't all have the same set of concerns, and no two people will look at something exactly the same way. Take a simple example: Give two people a glass with some water in it. One will describe it as 'half full', the other as 'half empty'. Then again, the same person will one day describe it one way at a certain time and the opposite way another. What are we saying? Well, simply that people are not neat. They do not think and behave according to formulas. Everyone is very different.

'Well, yes, state the obvious!' you might be thinking, but the reason I'm labouring this point a little is so that we avoid thinking there are set 'needs' to which we can give set solutions. Now with that in mind we can begin to look—in as general a way as time and space allows—at a few examples of 'needs'.

Put a bunch of Christians in a room together and ask them what made them first respond to Jesus and you'll get a huge variety of answers. Some will say they recognised they were sinners and needed forgiveness. Others will say because of their fear of dying, whilst some might say because of the hope for heaven. Some will say they began to explore Jesus out of fear of the unknown, some because they had a feeling that there must be something more to life; some because they heard God was a loving father; others because they were impressed by what they saw of a church community. Some knew deep down that they had done wrong things and felt guilt and shame. Many came looking for love or inner peace, then others because they grasped the idea that Jesus suffered and died to save them. Some will say they don't know, but when they hear all the other reasons they recognise that, yes, several of these ring true.

We can take a look at a few more of these in depth and, in some cases, hint at the way a person might begin to respond to Jesus as they explore the possibility of him meeting their need. Remember though, the last thing we want is to go down the road of 'pat' answers. So let's see 'people', not 'issues' and let's concentrate on meeting people, not needs.

Rachael has a feeling that there must be more to life. Whilst she wouldn't describe it as a 'trouble', she's aware that she's been nagged by this suspicion for as long as she can remember. Sometimes it just hangs around, sometimes it seems to disappear, but very often, given space and time she'll find herself battling with big concepts: life, meaning, the universe and everything in it. Sometimes she finds herself wondering where she fits in. What does her day-to-day existence mean? What is it all for? Rachel lets her imagination run. She wonders if, after all, we are each plugged into the 'Matrix' and the physical lives we think we see are nothing more than illusions? What if there is a bigger picture out there that she's missing. She's looking for Morpheus, she's looking for someone who can open up the real truth beyond this mode of existence.

Matt has a very hard life. He's been moved from one foster home to another and now he's living on the streets. He has no family to love him and no friends he can trust. It's every man for himself on the streets. Sometimes he's beaten up. Sometimes he's abused. He sees others like him die through drug addiction and fears that he might go the same way. He wonders if anyone would notice anyway. He's perpetually cold and hungry and the scars on his body are superficial in comparison to those inside. Sometimes he wonders about death. Surely it would be better than this. What if there is a heaven? He hopes there is. He longs for it to be true. What if someone could show him Jesus by meeting his practical needs. What if he could begin to explore his dreams about heaven; if he could discover the prophecy of Isaiah who spoke of a time when God would 'wipe every tear from every face'. What if he could hear about Jesus' promise of heaven... no tears, sadness, sorrow... only laughter and love and your loved ones around you again. Jesus said 'I am going to prepare a place for you, and will come back and get you.' Can Matt ignore this?

TALK BACK

Shaun: I've made a big mistake John, and it's like it's haunting me. I can't get the images out of my head.

John: Slow down. Just tell me what happened.

Shaun: Well, it's over a year ago now. I was over at my mate's house. We were playing a computer game, then he turned it off and got onto the internet. It turned out he was accessing a porn site. We were both just laughing, but I knew straight away I shouldn't be looking. It was like we couldn't turn it off though. In the end his mum came home, so we quickly went back to the game. Ever since I've kept seeing those pictures in my head.

John: Have you talked to your friend about it?

Shaun: No, but I know he's still looking at the site. The other day he was bragging about another one he's found. I don't even want to tell you what it has on it.

John: This is serious Shaun. For a start it's illegal and your friend and his family could be heading for big trouble. But look what it's doing to you.

Shaun: I know. And the thing I really hate is sometimes I deliberately remember, like I want to see the images again. If I wasn't so scared of it being traced, I'd have probably got onto the site from my PC. I hate myself for it. I feel somehow guilty and ashamed.

John: What do you want to do about it?

Shaun: I don't know really, that's why I'm telling you. You talk a lot about Jesus. I guess that's your job really, but do you think he can really help me?

John: This shame and guilt is really eating you up. Let me show you what the Bible says about it. The first letter of John talks a lot about what it means to be a child of Christ. I know you've heard before how part of choosing to follow Christ is recognising that you are a sinner (that you've done things that separate you from God) and that Jesus can forgive you and make you acceptable to God.

Shaun: Yeah, I had that drummed into me when my parents used to drag me along to church. I guess that's why I'm feeling the way I do then. This horrible dirty feeling inside...I suppose that's because of sin?

John: Probably. You've been coming to the youth club for a while now and meeting with friends who know Jesus. I suspect you're beginning to want to know more about him aren't you?

Shaun: Yeah, I guess so. Let's not get too carried away with it though.

John: Well, I have a feeling Jesus is already at work in your life and that's why you're becoming more aware and more troubled by shame.

Shaun: Maybe. But what do I do about it?

John: The key is that you don't have to continue to feel this way. Right now you're acutely aware of your sin *because you're full of shame and guilt. Such recognition is a big step. 1 John 8–9 says, 'If we say we have no sin, we are fooling ourselves, and the truth is not in us. But if we confess our sins, he will forgive our sins, because we can trust God to do what is right. He will cleanse us from all the wrongs we have done'.*

Shaun: *Yeah, but I'm not sure I want to make some big declaration about becoming a Christian. I don't want to be thought of as one of those geeks.*

John: *Let's not cloud the issue with all that Shaun. The passage I just showed you tells you what you need to do. If you're really interested, the Bible is full of this promise. Hebrews 10:22 '...let us come near to God with a sincere heart and a sure faith, because we have been made free from a guilty conscience, and our bodies have been washed with pure water.' You don't have to feel the guilt of what you did because God can, and will forgive you for it. Imagine being 'cleansed', being thoroughly cleaned.*

Shaun: *It sounds good. I might give it a try. Let me think about it for a while.*

John: *Sure, you know you can always come and talk again.*

Sarah needs to be part of something. She's moved schools and she misses her old gang. When she was with them she felt like she really belonged. She felt like she was someone special. At least they understood her. They felt the same about things. Now she feels she's alone. She's made a few friends, but it's not the same. They're all very different. They talk different, dress different, listen to different music and seem to want different things. Sarah longs to belong to something, to have somewhere to go where she is known, loved, appreciated; where she can meet with people who share similar dreams, aspirations, expectations. She's beginning to wonder about Julie. She seems really nice. Last week Julie introduced her to some of her friends. They were obviously very special friends. They all go to the same church and seem pretty excited by it. Sarah wonders what it is about the church that makes them so enthusiastic. She wonders if she might try it one day. At least it would be a way of meeting more people.

Andrew is anxious. He's stressed out about his exam next week. If he doesn't pass it he might not be able to carry on with the course. If he can't carry on with the course he might not be able to do the 'A' Level. If he can't do the 'A' Level he won't be able to go to university and if he can't go to university, well, he'll never get the job he wants. Without the job he won't earn the money to go travelling and to buy the car. But then maybe he won't get to do that anyway. Maybe there will be a war that changes everything. Maybe he'll be diagnosed with cancer, maybe, maybe, what if, what then…Andrew's head is buzzing. He feels like it's always that way. He can't sit still because there's always something going on in his head. There's always stuff to do. His sister is the same. She says she needs to find 'inner peace'. She practises Yoga. It seems to work. Well, for half an hour at least. Andrew thinks maybe he'll try it. Then again, there are just so many uncertainties. Maybe he should start studying horoscopes instead. He just wants some reassurance, some sense of destiny.

Psalm 139

> Lord, you have examined me and know all about me…
> You know my thoughts before I think them…
> You know thoroughly everything I do…
> You made my whole being; you formed me in my
> mother's body…
> All the days planned for me were written in your book
> before I was one day old.

For Vivian 'brokenness' is a way of life. Her father left her mother when he found out she was pregnant. Throughout Vivian's childhood there was a stream of would-be fathers. Each would arrive with the promise of love and security, only to depart, leaving Vivian and her mother alone again. One day, in a rage, her mother lashed out, 'He would have stayed with me if not for you!' Vivian became involved with a boy when she was twelve. He took her innocence and left. After a string of others, Vivian found herself pregnant and alone, at sixteen. She was a broken person who understood 'love' only as sex and abandonment. Vivian is looking for acceptance. She's looking for unconditional love that will never fail her. She's looking to be loved as a child should be loved. She's looking for someone who will accept her no matter what, brokenness and all.

John misses his Dad. At least he thinks he does. John never knew him long enough before he died. He knows about his Dad because of his mum's stories. He imagines his Dad must have been really special and it saddens him that he has to 'imagine'. Sometimes he wishes mum would marry again so he could have someone he could call Dad. It goes beyond football games and fishing trips. That would be good, but John thinks if he had a father he'd feel more certain about life. He'd have someone to go to when he's stuck with things, when he's worried, when he feels lost. He suspects his father would never let him down, would love him unconditionally.

You probably know Rachel, Matt, Shaun, Sarah, Andrew, Vivian, John…You may be them. At least, you'll probably identify with some of their feelings, some of their 'needs'. You may have things you want to say to them, things you want to show them. But be careful, remember all they need you to be is a friend.

> *I will help them connect their story*
> *Meet them in their fears*
> *Wondering*
> *Searching*
> *Turmoil*
> *Sadness*
> *Anxiety*
> *Setbacks*
> *Poverty*
> *Hunger*
> *Longing*
> *Shame*
> *Guilt*
> *Loneliness*
> *I will meet them when they feel they have no need*
> *I pray that they will connect to Jesus as their*
> *Friend*
> *Saviour*
> *Lord*

Now, a big word of warning. We've talked about everyone having different needs and noted the fact that this will influence the way they may begin to seek Jesus. However, let me stress that God's story is not a 'need-based' thing. Many New Age philosophies have sprung up around this idea, creating 'pick and mix' kind of religions: 'I will take this bit from here and another bit from there because that's what works for me. That's what makes me feel good.' No. God is God, irrespective of us. Jesus came to save each one of us, whether we recognise it or not. Truth is truth, whether we accept it or not. So, what am I saying here? Well, simply that everyone 'needs' Jesus, no matter how good or bad life is. You've probably got some friends who show no interest in getting to know Jesus, simply because they feel they have no 'need' for him. It's also the case that people will often have needs that are not obvious or even apparent to them, never mind us. Take, for example, the story in Mark chapter 2. The paralysed man's friends lowered him through the roof of the house where Jesus was speaking. They did this because he had a very obvious need for physical healing. That's what he and his friends thought was his biggest need. However, look at Jesus' response. What he saw first was a different, he believed much bigger, need. He said to the man, 'Your sins are forgiven'. Now that was a shock. It certainly wasn't what the man's friends expected, nor the onlookers who were hungry for a miraculous display.

Let's remember what we are told very clearly in the Bible about our need for Jesus. **Romans 3:22 reminds us**

> God makes people right with himself through their faith in Christ, because all people are the same; all have sinned and are not good enough for God's glory, and all need to be made right with God by his grace, which is a free gift.

See, there's no grey area here, is there? Look at the number of times the word 'all' appears in this verse. The Bible is very clear that no matter who or what we are, each and everyone of us needs Jesus to become 'right' (that is, back in the relationship he intended) with God.

There are many mysteries in Christianity, but there are also many certainties.

This is one of them. Indeed, this is the one that may give you the most motivation to share God's story with as many people as you can. What is the alternative to choosing God, to accepting his free gift of grace that cleans us of our sin? Well, the Bible, in Romans 6:23, tells us that, 'When people sin, they earn what sin pays—death.' No compromise here then! Thankfully, that verse continues, 'But God gives us a free gift—life for ever in Christ Jesus our Lord.' Jesus said the same thing. Read what he says about himself in John 10:10, 'I came to give life—life in all its fullness.' We know this. We know we have a choice. We know the consequences of making the wrong choice (or for ignoring the message and not bothering to make a choice at all). Let this be your motivation to pray for your friends, even the ones you feel aren't interested in God's story. You won't fail to have an impact on them. Trust God's timing. Trust the changing of their hearts to the Holy Spirit. All you need to do is be a 'storyteller' through which God's story can be revealed.

PART 3: GOD'S STORY
CHAPTER 5: **THE TRUTH OF THE STORY**

In chapter 4 we began to explore some of the different reasons why people might become interested in learning more about Jesus. One of the main purposes of this was to emphasise to ourselves the fact that not everyone is the same as us. Even if we speak the same language, we inevitably end up putting our own slant on a conversation or experience, just because of who we are. This is something Jesus knew only too well. Remember earlier we looked at the way he treated everyone he met as an individual, according to their need. Jesus knew how to get on the same wavelength of every person he encountered. Read for yourself and see if you can understand the differences in, for example, the woman caught in adultery (John 8), Nicodemus (John 3), Zacchaeus (Luke 19), the rich man (Luke 18), the Samaritan woman at the well (John 4).

The reason three story living works is because it communicates God's story in the most natural way, through developing relationships. God's story does not end. It is the best story ever written and it is living, breathing and continual in its revelation (as long as we ask for it to be revealed). It is there because of us, and in spite of us.

Ultimately, God's story provokes a response. It means choices. In all our relationships, and throughout life, we're required to make choices, regardless of whether we're particularly conscious of that fact or not. Let's now look at how we might help our friends as they start to want to make a response to Jesus. Remember, however, that we're not necessarily talking about one big choice here that changes everything. As I've tried to stress throughout this book, coming to know Jesus is a process, not a formula. It's an individual journey, a relationship being explored, nurtured and developed. So again, as you see your friend begin to engage in God's story, do not take this as your green light to put on your preaching hat and try to explain Christian apologetics. Don't suddenly change the way you talk. Remember, most of our friends have no background in church and therefore have no notion of the language that's often used when talking about faith. Tell a friend they must repent of their sin and be washed in the redeeming blood of the sacrificial lamb, and you'll have them running for cover!

TALK BACK

Timothy: I've been having a few discussions with Simon recently about God and what I believe. When do you think I should tell him he needs to repent of his sins and ask Jesus to come into his life.

John: I don't know. It depends if you think he's ready.

Timothy: Pardon?

John: Well, is Simon hung up on the fact that he is a sinner? Does he understand how to ask Jesus into his life and what the implications of doing that are?

Timothy: No, but I'm going to explain it to him.

John: And when he legs it out of the room and doesn't call you again...?

Timothy: You're saying he's probably not ready?

John: *I'm saying he probably doesn't need to be preached at about things he has no concept of.*

Timothy: *But how will he know, if I don't tell him?*

John: *I'm not saying don't tell him. But be careful of shutting down the relationship by saying the wrong thing in the wrong way at the wrong time.*

Timothy: *I get that, but surely he needs to understand the basics of Christianity.*

John: *Yes, when the time is right and he's in a position to make a response to them. Take me for example. I first encountered something of the Gospel when I was sixteen. I didn't fully understand it, but I bought into the concept that there was a God who accepted me. That was big stuff. Then, the idea of someone suffering on my behalf really blew my mind. It was so powerful to me that I had to make a response. Looking back now, I realise how little I knew and understood at that time, but nonetheless I had made a very real and authentic response to Jesus. The little bit of God's story that I did grasp started me on a journey that would change my life forever. And the little bit I had, gave me a huge hunger to find out more.*

Timothy: *So where does this leave me with Simon?*

John: *It leaves you being his friend. It leaves the Holy Spirit working in Simon's life and him becoming more curious about Jesus. It leaves him asking questions and you doing lots of listening. It also leaves you living out your life with Jesus as your priority.*

Timothy: *So, no explanations, no decisions?*

John: *If he asks, then that's your golden opportunity. But, as I've said, be careful how you handle it because the last thing you want is to scare him off because he can't handle what you're saying. Answer his questions naturally* *through your own story. Remember, you're not a preacher or an 'evangelist', but you are Simon's friend and you are a witness for Jesus.*

Timothy: *Okay, I think I get where you're coming from.*

John: *The more you engage in the debate, the more Simon will ask questions. Be sensitive to the guidance of the Holy Spirit so that you'll know when the time is right to talk to him about the choices you've made. With every small piece you gently reveal, Simon will want more. Consider also whether it might be a good idea to introduce him to an Alpha course or bring him along to one of our events. Just remember to let him set the timing.*

What is the most special thing about God's story? Well, I'd say it is the fact that we are part of it. Our own lives have cosmic significance, because we have a 'relationship' with God through Jesus. Just think about that. Mind-blowing isn't it? Let me also say that if you engage in sharing this story, your life will never be the same again. That is, your journey will be changed in a way that you will never fully understand until you start to do it. You'll find yourself with an excitement, enthusiasm and confidence that makes you want to share more of God's story with more people.

We've talked so much about 'relationships', and this should really make sense when you consider that God's story, itself, is relationship-based. It is built around our relationship with him. As with any other relationship, we should see it as a journey on which we discover new things, the more we spend time together. When we get married to someone we don't know all about them. All we know is that we love the bit we do know, so much so that we can make a commitment to them and start a journey together. Five, ten and twenty years on, that relationship is still developing. That's the way it is in discovering Jesus.

So the point I'm pressing here is that you don't need to know everything about God's story to become part of it. That is, you don't need to know the

PART 3: GOD'S STORY

ins and outs of 'Christianity' to become a 'follower of Jesus Christ', so why try to explain everything all at once to your friend?

The woman at the well knew only that Jesus knew her story (John 4). The blind man knew only that somehow this man Jesus could make him see (Mark 10). The old woman knew only that if she touched the hem of Jesus' coat she could be healed from her bleeding (Matthew 9). Nicodemus knew only that he had to be born again (John 3). All these things are packed full of revelations waiting to be explored, but at the time they were just glimpses of knowledge and understanding. The point is, they were big enough to provoke a response. Also take, for example, the thief on the cross next to Jesus as he was crucified. Talk about cutting it fine! It's doubtful that he knew anything much about Jesus' teaching. What he did know, though, was that he had lived a sinful life, that death was a just punishment and that Jesus was on a very different ticket. Just think of the drama of that scene. Here was a man who was probably moments away from death—from separation from God, or eternal life with him. In those moments he recognised his sinful life and the punishment he deserved. It's hard to know what he expected might happen. What we do know is that he recognised Jesus as his potential saviour (after death), and Jesus, in turn, gave him his 'salvation', as he said, 'I tell you the truth, today you will be with me in paradise.' (Luke 23:40–43).

Now might be a good time to actually take a look at God's story. Remember, we're not doing this so that we can trot out the full Bible story the minute someone shows a glimmer of interest in God. Rather, we're reminding ourselves of the story we are part of and the relationship we hope to reveal to those who connect with us.

God's story is there in the Bible. Now, unless you're highly adept in the art of speed reading, it's going to take you a while to dig through it all, so let me do a very quick resume...

In Genesis chapter 1, we learn that God created the world, including all the living creatures and man and woman (that's us). Everything was hunky-dory. He made us really special so we could enjoy a loving relationship with him and with each other. God loved us, we loved God. Perfect. But, by the end of chapter 3 we'd messed things up big style. We'd done the one thing God told us not to and 'sin' was introduced into the relationship, which turned it really sour. We turned our back on God. Pretty much the rest of the Old Testament is full of stories of God trying to help man and woman out again. You see, that beautiful relationship was broken, but God still loved us and he kept giving opportunities and calling us back to that relationship. By the end of the Old Testament God must have felt like he was banging his head against a brick wall, so he decided it was time to make the ultimate sacrifice, to give it his best shot and come down to earth himself to sort out the situation (actually, he must have suspected he'd have to do this all along, because he makes numerous undercover references to it throughout the Old Testament).

This is where the New Testament starts, with a whole new relationship. God came to earth in the form of his son, Jesus. In the Gospel stories we're told who Jesus was and what he was like. Some took notice of him. Many didn't. Either way, God chose to make the ultimate sacrifice. Even though man and woman still turned their back on him, he chose to provide a way for us to get back into that proper relationship with him. That's what the cross is all about. Jesus took what we deserved, the death penalty. He paid the price for that initial sin, and for all the sins after it, and all the sins to come (yes, that includes ours, the ones we did today, and the ones we will inevitably do tomorrow!). The good news is that Jesus dying was all part of the plan. He died a very real death, but three days later he rose to life, proving that he was, and is, God, and that death has no hold on him. After that, all we had to do was believe in him and we would be back in the relationship that God first intended (John 3:16).

So that's God's story. Here it's very crudely summarised, but hopefully it will help you see that God's biggest concern in his whole story is his relationship with us. Throughout history, he continues to pursue those he loves, those he intended to love him. Yes, your little life is connected to Almighty God, the maker of heaven and earth, in a most loving and passionate way. When we realise how his story impacts our story, we also become aware of the privileged position we are in to fulfil the purposes of God. We begin to

PART 3: GOD'S STORY

look at our relationships with an eternal perspective. What do I mean here? Well, simply that my little life—just living it out in openness to Jesus—could help change my friend's life forever and have an impact for God's kingdom.

Let's have a look at some ways you might naturally connect your friend's story to God's story, just through everyday interaction. Remember, the key thing we're doing here is revealing Jesus by talking about ourselves and, if the time is right, perhaps drawing on the stories Jesus himself used.

'I'm just terrified', says Sarah. *You're chatting about the state of the world and the possibilities of war. 'I mean, it's not like war used to be', she says. 'Chemical weapons, dirty bombs, nuclear stuff. If we end up at war it really could be the end of the world.' You let the conversation develop, agreeing that you too are fearful of the suffering that war can bring. But you know you can also share with Sarah the deeper hope that you have that helps put your fear into perspective. 'I'm scared too', you might say, 'but I know the end of the world won't come until God decides.' Sarah might be a little surprised by your comment, but then she's also always been aware of the sense of peace you seem to have in difficult situations. She asks you why you're so sure about God. From here, the conversation can develop in all manner of ways. The key thing to remember is to keep it real. Don't try to explain theology or get embroiled in apologetics. You're not trying to prove God exists. Sarah has asked why you are sure about God. So tell her your story. Tell her what having a relationship with Jesus means to you. Be honest. She knows you're not a super human, so don't pretend you are and don't make out that life is perfect because of Jesus. If you do, the next time she sees you losing your temper, you'll discredit everything you've said. Instead, just let the conversation weave it's natural way. It may be that it doesn't get much further, but Sarah will not forget the fact that your inner peace comes from a very real trust in what appears to be a very real and loving God.*

Now this, itself, is enough to blow her mind for a while, and chances are Sarah is going to want to revisit this idea with you another time. Perhaps she's never really even thought about the existence of God, and if she has, she's considered him a far off phenomena that has little relevance or bear-

ing on her life. To hear that you feel you can call him 'Father', talk with him every day and trust your destiny to him is going to be a huge point of interest for her.

You're talking with Melinda. *You've just watched 'Lord of the Rings' together and she's scared to go out of the room alone because she's freaked out by the scenes with the Orcs. 'They're gross', she says. 'It reminds me of my great granny who used to talk about hell all the time. She used to terrify me. I still have nightmares about me going to hell and being trapped forever'. You let her talk a little more, while you quietly ask God to guide your conversation. Then Melinda says, 'Do you think hell exists?' Oh no, it's a biggy. How on earth do you cope with that one?*

Don't panic. Don't try wracking your brains for what the Bible teaches about hell. Instead, it might be appropriate to open up for Melinda the assurance Jesus gives of eternal life. John 3:16 is an obvious place to start. 'God loved the world so much that he gave his one and only son, so that whoever believes in him may not be lost but will have eternal life.' This verse is a great one to remember because it really does sum up the good news of God's story. There's loads to talk about here—God's love, Jesus' sacrifice, what 'believing' entails... But be careful. The last thing Melinda needs is you preaching. Be sensitive to what she's asked you in the light of what you know of her. If you feel she is receptive, you might reveal your belief that the eternal life promised in John 3:16 means the 'hell' she fears need not be an issue. Eternal life means life everlasting, safe and secure with God. You might then go on to talk about Jesus' promise of life in all its fullness (John 10:10) and open up for her the fact that 'fullness' of life is available for her right now, on earth. She doesn't even have to wait until after death. That should set your conversation down a really interesting track as you begin to share with her what it means in your everyday life.

Chris thinks it would be a good idea to practise a religion. *He's beginning to suspect there's something more to this world and religion might be an answer. 'Some of the really cool rap artists are Muslims, I might check it out', he* says casually. Now at this point, you might be itching to get into some heated debate about the virtues of Christianity above other religions. But be careful. Don't blow your friendship with Chris by suddenly becoming dogmatic and over assertive. Remember, this isn't about winning arguments, or 'persuading' Chris to see things your way. It's more than doubtful that he's suddenly going to say, 'Okay, you're right, I'll be a Christian then'. Let him talk more. Remember what we said back in chapter 3 about listening, asking questions, letting conversations unfold and all that stuff. You might ask him why he thinks he needs 'religion'. That will bring up some interesting things and it will be helpful for him to explore what he thinks 'religion' is and what it can do for him. Perhaps another friend might butt in saying he believes religion is the cause of a lot of trouble in the world, or that it's just a way of keeping us in control, following rules and regulations. This is always an area for heated debate, but it's really best avoided because it's not really the issue here. You might decide that you can slightly guide the conversation at this point, as you say that what you believe has more to do with 'love' than rules. Remember, you're not arguing the corner for 'Christianity', you're just revealing a little of what you believe and what it means in your life.

If you feel the time is right, and Chris is sufficiently interested, you could invite him to look at Mark 12:28–34 with you (actually, you probably wouldn't whip out your Bible, but rather just tell him the story). Here Jesus is put on the spot as the people ask him what he believes is the most important commandment. That's like them asking 'What is the most important thing in life?' Jesus' answer is 'love'. Now this might take Chris aback a little. Perhaps he was expecting to hear something more like…'Go to church every Sunday', 'Give all your money away', 'Be nice to old ladies and children', 'Watch Songs of Praise every week'…

The conversation could develop in many ways from here. You might find yourselves exploring what it means to 'love' and be 'loved'. This is why all we've looked at about building relationships and knowing your friend is important. If Chris has a terrible background of abuse, he will have a very different idea about 'love' to someone who has a loving family. Either way, Chris will have specific ideas about the concept of love and, hopefully, you will be able to sensitively share with him what the love of God means to you. Remember also what we've said about drawing from Jesus' story when you feel the time is right. Jesus used the story of the prodigal son to illustrate the phenomenal love God has for his children, even though it is not deserved. Or perhaps the story of the Good Samaritan is a good one to tell here. Remember, it was the 'religious' man who walked by and left the Samaritan for dead. Real 'love' was demonstrated by the man who sacrificed his own comfort for a stranger.

Then there's Jason. You know he's going through a really tough time. His father abandoned him when he was very young. Since then his mother has had several boyfriends. He's told you before how one of them used to regularly beat both Jason and his mother. A year ago, another man moved into the home and you've seen Jason become close to him. You went with them both to watch football games and he seemed like a really cool guy. Then, last week, there was a mighty row and the man moved out. Jason is now feeling abandoned again by a man he thought he'd like to call Dad. You don't know what to say. You've sat with him in silence. You've talked for hours. Then he asks you how you deal with the fact that you don't have a dad living at home. You ponder for a while, and talk about your struggles, but you can also talk to him about your relationship with your father God— the unending love he has for you, the way you can rely on him when everyone else lets you down, the way you trust that he has your best interests at heart. If it seems Jason is really curious to pursue the conversation in this way, you might share a story Jesus told. Remember the one about the lost sheep? The shepherd never gives up on the missing sheep, but searches and searches until he can find it, put it on his shoulders and bring it back home. You might end up getting your Bible out and showing him how precious he is to God (read Psalm 139, for example). Ultimately, by sharing the way you feel about God and the promises in the Bible, you can show Jason that God wants him to be his child. Point him towards John 1:12–13. 'But to all who did accept him and believe in him he gave the right to become children of God. They did not become his children in any human way—by any human parents or human desire. They were born of God.'

Do you see what I'm getting at with these four scenarios? They're all natural conversations that flow out of different circumstances. Okay, so I've done a bit of engineering, but as you spend time with people you'll find that they are interested in what you've got to say. Questions will be asked, but this rarely means that you should dive in with a full explanation of God, life and the universe. We've already said this, but it's important. Remember to try to be aware of your friend's point of need. Why have they asked you a certain question? Should you try to give an answer, or should you ask another question back so you can reveal more of the real issue at heart. How should you begin to answer the question? Should you start with God, Jesus, yourself or your friend? These are all open-ended questions because, at the end of the day, there is no right answer. Remember, no formulas, no rules, just relationships.

All the scenarios we've looked at leave huge scope for development. It's unlikely that Melinda, Sarah, Chris and Jason would make a commitment to Jesus immediately after these conversations. However, you will have helped them along in a journey of discovery which may have begun months or years ago. Traditional teaching on evangelism often has you pushing your friend towards a 'decision' for Jesus, but three story living encourages us to not get hung up with 'closing the deal'. Remember, if you've spent time cultivating relationships, the last thing you need to do is blow it by pushing your friend into something they're not ready for. It might even be that our four friends here wait years before they explore Jesus further. At that time, you might not

Relationships aren't tidy.

We can spend a lot of time with a person then, for whatever reason, we might not see them for a while. But usually when we meet again the relationship carries on where it left off. That's the way it is with our stories and conversations. We can leave stories at the beginning or in the middle, just as easily as at the end. Wherever we left them they will live on and develop more the next time we pick them up, or until they are picked up by someone else for that matter!

be around, but you can be sure that God will have placed other people in their path to continue their journey with them.

On the other hand, it may well be that you have the privilege of helping your friend really explore Jesus in an active way. As parts of God's story begin to ring true with him or her you can expect to be asked more and more questions. That's because an authentic glimpse of God causes a growing hunger to see more. You'll find yourself talking more openly about Jesus and the implications that following him has on your life. As your friend begins to explore God's story, he or she will probably ask a lot about how you handle things in the light of God's story. For example, 'You seem to have a different approach towards some things, why is that?' 'How do you cope with being the only one when you're surrounded by people who don't believe in the same way?' 'How do you stay strong in what you believe?' 'Does God really help you in everyday life?' You should be excited by these kind of questions. They are all positive. They are all part of your friend's growing intrigue in God's story. Some of them you will handle better than others, but because they are very personal questions all you need to do is speak from your own experience and your own heart. Just be yourself and you won't need to worry about 'right' or 'wrong' answers.

As you listen to your friend's story and help him or her explore God's story through their questions, you'll find you're also learning more of it yourself. Travelling with your friend becomes a meaningful and very significant part of your own journey with God. The key thing to bear in mind is the recognition that you are both part of God's story and must remain connected to it. Remember, Jesus is your Lord and Saviour. He's also your best friend. So talk about him. You'll find that it is 'Jesus' and the implication of him in your life that fascinates people. It's not religious concepts. Don't talk about 'faith', 'spirituality', 'Christianity', 'theology'.

Talk about Jesus.

Who he was.

Who he is.

What he is to you.

TALK BACK

Katy: I'm reading this stuff John, and I understand what's being said, but for some reason I just can't bring myself to talk about Jesus when I'm trying to explain Christianity.

John: Read again Katy. Why are you trying to explain Christianity? Think about what you've just said. Jesus is Christianity.

Katy: I know, but it just feels weird saying 'Jesus'.

John: You're not the first person to admit this, but when we do nothing more than talk about 'faith', 'religion', 'Christianity', 'spirituality' and all such words, we're really missing the heart of the message. And face it Katy, who's interested in that stuff? We've heard it all before. The church has been preaching concepts for hundreds of years!

Katy: So...?

John: So, people aren't interested in concepts, belief systems and rituals. They're interested in people. More and more I find that people are fascinated by the person of Jesus. They want to know about him.

Katy: So I should really try to talk about him as if I were talking about my best friend?

John: Exactly. 'Jesus' is a very special name. It means 'Salvation', the one who came to save. The more you treasure your relationship with Jesus, the more his name will feel precious on your lips. I really believe there's power in his name.

Katy: Wow. That sounds big.

John: It's a question of confidence Katy. Remember, your friends want to know about your relationship with Jesus, not the rituals you follow. So talk about him, and enjoy it!

It is Jesus who is at the heart of God's story. Jesus is God's story. Indeed, God's story throughout history was building to that great cosmic event which is Christ on the cross. So too, our story is given that we may also come to this point, the foot of the cross. We may come to Jesus because we realise that the Gospel meets our 'need', however, we must also come to the point where we realise that what Christ did on the cross has significance far beyond that. More than meeting need, our acceptance of Christ as our saviour changes our heart. This may not be what we discover first as we begin to travel with him, in fact, it probably won't be, but, ultimately, it is an essential and critical part of our journey.

In all our listening, conversations and relationship building, our desire is that our friend gets on the road to begin a journey with Christ.

Where they get on the road may well be different to where you joined it. That does not matter. The big thing is that they encounter Christ so that, when the time is right, they will be able to make those critical choices towards him.

Now, chances are you've been to many events or evangelistic meetings where there has been an 'altar call' (that is, people have been invited to make a public statement—usually by going to the front, or standing up—declaring that they want to become a Christian). When this happens you are led through a series of steps explaining what you're about to do, which then culminates in what is often called a 'sinners' or a 'believers' prayer.

TALK BACK

Nick: *I'm so frustrated for Michael. I thought he'd really gone for it when we went to that meeting, but look at him now.*

John: *What do you mean?*

Nick: Well he was telling his mates it meant nothing to him really. And yet he went forward, he prayed. He seemed so excited. He was even crying at the end, so I was sure the Holy Spirit was working in him.

John: Don't doubt that he was Nick, but sadly I've seen this all too often. It was a great meeting wasn't it. The music was great. The preaching was strong. It was hard to resist the call to the front afterwards.

Nick: You're not saying it was all phoney, just sales technique.

John: No, not at all. For many people in that meeting it would be the beginning of a very real walk with God. But Michael has obviously gone the other way. He's probably really confused about what happened. He may be trying to discredit it, but I'm sure he won't have forgotten it. In fact he may be in a bit of turmoil deep down.

Nick: Yeah, he seemed really quite angry when I tried to talk with him about it later.

John: The trouble is, he was pushed into steps he didn't understand and wasn't ready to make. We've now got a repair job on our hands.

Nick: What do you mean?

John: Well, for a start, don't imagine that God has abandoned Michael. He won't let him go. We must continue to pray for him and start to re-build the relationship. It might be difficult, because he now associates me and you with the meeting and all that went on there; but if we can concentrate on just being ourselves, on being his friend and on not pushing anything I think we'll find that he wants to hang out again. Concentrate on being his friend so he can continue to reveal his story to you. Eventually you'll find him becoming interested in yours again.

Sadly, we all probably know a number of people who genuinely believe they have made a commitment by going through a series of steps, only to find that some time down the road it means nothing to them. (That's not to discredit this practice. For some, the evangelistic meeting is a significant part of their journey and a public declaration is exactly what they need to go through. It can also be the case that some are so blown away by the message that they really do sign up there and then to following Jesus because of what they've heard and find themselves with an authentic, ongoing relationship with God.) This is why all we've said about three story living stands so well. It's about 'story' and 'process', 'relationships' and 'development', not steps. Usually when a person grasps hold of what Jesus did for them on the cross and comes to him seeking his forgiveness, the chances are they have already been journeying with him for some time.

However, that is not to say that the so called 'believers' or 'sinners' prayer is not valid. Far from it. The Bible gives us very clear guidance on what we must 'do' to accept God's promise of forgiveness for sins and eternal life. John 3:16 lays it out very simply. Mark's gospel in chapter 1:15 records that Jesus, very early in his ministry, instructed, 'Change your hearts and lives and believe the Good News!' 'Change your hearts' is a modern way of saying 'repent' (which you might see depending on which version of the Bible you're looking at). This change of heart ultimately means that you say you are sorry for your sin, you really mean it, and you commit to turning away from it (at least, you commit to wanting to turn away from it. Remember, it is Christ in us that transforms us, not our own strength). This all relies, of course, on you coming to some understanding of your sin—your need for a 'change of heart', in the first place.

Believing in the Good News means believing in the Gospel, signing up to God's story. What is God's story? Well, we've already said, it is the cross of Christ and the fact that his death on that cross means forgiveness for us so that we can be back in a right relationship with God. Indeed, Paul, in 1 Corinthians 2:2, tells us in no uncertain terms what the Good News hinged on: 'Christ and his death on the cross'. Let's take a look at how some of the early believers responded to this. Read Acts 2. (Be aware that the medium of the message here is slightly different to what we've been looking at in three story living. Acts 2 sees Peter with his preaching hat on, whereas we're looking at natural conversation and interaction between friends. However, the 'message' is the same.) Peter and the other apostles are telling the story of Jesus to a large crowd that had gathered in Jerusalem. They have just been filled with the Holy Spirit and Peter's teaching is powerful and authoritative. In verse 36, Peter concludes his story telling them, 'God has made Jesus—the man you nailed to the cross—both Lord and Christ.' Imagine the emotion, the horror of the realisation, even. In fact, we don't have to imagine. We are told, 'When the people heard this, they felt guilty and asked Peter and the other disciples, "What shall we do?"' They knew they had to respond. Now, if we're revealing this message in a natural, low key environment as we're chatting with a friend, there's unlikely to be the same drama in the scene. However, your friend is beginning to understand God's story and, just like the people in Acts 2, they will realise that they need to make a response, they need to do something about it. We may journey for some time, making moves nearer to Jesus through all the choices we make, but, ultimately, we must either reject or accept him. Peter is clear about what the people had to do. In verse 38 he says to them, 'Change your hearts and lives and be baptised, each one of you, in the name of Jesus Christ for the forgiveness of your sins. And you will receive the gift of the Holy Spirit.'

Three story living will hopefully bring your friend to this point. As your relationship has grown they will have shared with you, watched you, listened to you, questioned you, debated with you. You will probably have invited them along to church events, festivals, meetings. They might have done an Alpha course and will have enjoyed getting to know more of Jesus and his story, all the time making decisions that lead him or her closer to the cross.

This is where a so-called 'believers prayer' is very helpful. It can be used as a commitment and as an acknowledgement to God, and to others, that your friend believes in Jesus; that he or she wants to change his or her life, and that he/she knows this can only be done through Jesus because only he can forgive sins. It is also a point at which they will accept the gift of the Holy Spirit to be a personal helper and guide. A brief note here in case you're about to get all tied up in the idea of 'baptism' and receiving the Holy

Spirit. First of all, baptism doesn't necessarily mean your friend has to instantly leg it to the nearest swimming pool for a full immersion. This may well come later, as a very positive and meaningful public declaration of their new life in Christ. For now, however, what is most important is that they make known their decision to follow him, simply by telling someone else. This someone may well be you, as you simply continue to talk together and share in your friend's new commitment. Secondly, rest assured that when a person makes a commitment in this way they are given the gift of the Holy Spirit. We know this, because we're told so in Acts 2:38. We may have a very real 'feeling' when this happens (remember the warm and fuzzy that Sharon talked about in our chapter 2 Talk Back?) Then again, we may not. Such an experience might happen years later, or it might be that we recognise the work of the Holy Spirit in our lives in a different way altogether. Either way, you can hold onto the promise that the Holy Spirit is in your life because you invited him to be there when you came to the cross and accepted Jesus.

There's nothing like the joy and enthusiasm of someone with a new hunger for God. At times, as you journey with them, you may feel you're running headlong into Jesus' arms yourself. You'll probably want to enlist the help

There is no formula to bring a person to Jesus.

Neither is there a particular prayer or set of 'magic' words. However, there are critical elements of God's story that need to be grasped and when this happens you might encourage your friend to use them as his or her prayer:

Tell Jesus you recognise that you don't know him but would like to get to know him. Say you are sorry and want to change your life. Tell Jesus you want to accept the forgiveness that only he can give. Ask him to give you the Holy Spirit so he can help you and be your guide.

When anyone asks these things, God promises that he will respond. (See John 5:24, 1 John 5:10–13, Romans 10:9–10 and many more similar verses throughout the New Testament.)

of other Christians, so be sure to invite your friend to church or to events where they can meet other followers of Jesus. This is where your friend can receive teaching and become part of the fellowship of believers and the worshipping body of Christ. However, don't imagine that at this point you step out and leave it to others. No, far from it. In fact, your relationship is now as important as it has ever been. Continue to pray for them. We've not mentioned this up to now, but the relationship you are building is actually what the Bible would refer to as 'discipleship'. So here we are, back at Matthew 28 again. 'So go and make followers of all people in the world.' Do you see? We're not told to make 'converts', we're told to make followers or 'disciples', as it's written in some Bible translations. This is what you've probably been doing from the moment you came into your friend's life. Now, long may that journey of discipleship continue.

PART 3: GOD'S STORY
CHAPTER 6: **JUST DO IT!**

'Once I began to listen sincerely, my heart was broken yet again for those around me. I came to see my friends as sheep without a shepherd. And I could not help telling them how Jesus came into my helplessness, how he shepherds me still and will shepherd them if they wish it.'

'And do they wish it?' the storyteller asked.

'They do indeed,' the young man replied. 'Not all, but many, and with all their hearts! As for those who do not yet wish to know Jesus as I do, I am committed to my relationship with them, to know them more. Above all, I am committed to my relationship with Jesus, to know him ever better and I believe that my continuing relationship with him will help me understand what part of God's story most graciously connects my friends with Jesus. In the meantime, I will feed the fruit of God's story in their lives.'

'Great!' said the storyteller. 'You have learned the three secrets. Now go in peace.'

Seeing the storyteller's words were true, the young man returned home excited and eager to tell the story of Jesus as never before.

Remember the final part of the story that opened this book? Hopefully you will now share the same sense of freedom and enthusiasm in your approach to telling God's story as the young man in the parable.

When we started our story, I assumed that, like lots of other friends, you were intimidated and fearful of the idea of talking to others about your faith. I assumed you believed 'evangelism' was something to be practised by those who knew the method and formula better than you. In thinking this way you have probably so far been successful in the art of comfortably dodging the issue. Was I right?

Hopefully, as we're at the end of my story, you'll now understand that we are all called to share God's story with others and that we do that most naturally and comfortably within the realms of our ongoing relationships. If you've already begun to do this you'll probably have tasted something of the excitement in realising that your life will never be the same again. Your journey will have moved on and you'll have recognised that, unless we are acutely aware of our own part in God's story, we are not in a good position to share it with others. In fact, chapter 2 should have left you doing a spiritual check-up and hopefully stoked your enthusiasm about using some of the tools God has given us to help our 'connections' with him on a daily basis.

If you've understood the purpose of this book, you'll now have blown apart the misconception that there is one way to share the Gospel and that you should push your friend through a set of steps and decisions at all costs. Instead, you'll recognise that everyone comes to Jesus in different ways and for different reasons and that getting to know him is an ongoing journey. You'll have stopped thinking of the Gospel as a set of facts to be remembered and communicated. Instead you'll be concentrating on communicating Jesus to real people whose lives do not work in formulas and lists. You'll be communicating in a way that recognises both you and your friend as complicated, untidy, changing, sometimes ambiguous and unreceptive to quick fixes, easy solutions and pat answers.

In all this you'll be feeling more comfortable in the knowledge that the timing is not your own. God is passionate about bringing his people back into a relationship with him and it is the Holy Spirit who creates the desire in a person to know Jesus. Your job then, is to provide the opportunity for that to happen. The best you can do for a friend is walk with them, 'disciple' them, pray for them and trust God to reveal more of his story through the working of the Holy Spirit.

Let's summarise this in a picture. Imagine three circles, representing three stories. One is God's story, the second is your story, and the third is another person's story. You are part of God's story, so your circles immediately overlap. As your relationship with him grows, more of your circle is merged into God's. You come across many people in the course of your story and as a certain person becomes a 'friend' their circle starts to move towards yours so that they overlap. Because all the time you are becoming more a part of God's circle you inevitably draw your friend's circle towards God's. Then, over a period of time, your friend's circle starts to move towards God's circle purely out of its own desire to see more of what it holds. This is three story evangelism. Three stories merged together, all God's story.

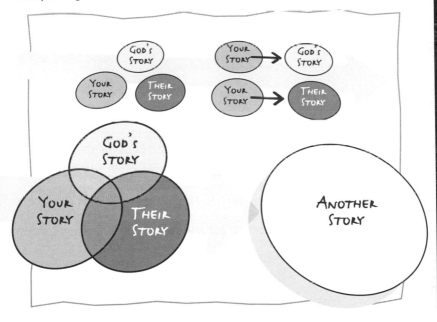

So what are you waiting for? Get out there and start living your story. One final word of encouragement. Just remember that God is extremely committed to using you and the web of relationships you weave together. You may get things wrong sometimes, in fact, you probably will, but you are not alone. You are part of God's story and who knows what part you're going to play in his divine plan? Be excited by this. For your friend, God's story might start with you. You never know who you might influence towards Jesus. You never know whose story is going to link to God's story because of it being linked to yours. So keep telling your story and down the line that's how you'll be making 'followers of all people in the world' (Matthew 28:19).

TALK BACK

Peter: I think I blew it again John.

John: What happened this time?

Peter: Well, I've been doing as you said and trying to concentrate on being a friend to the new girl in my class, Sally. It was all going really great until I said I was going to a 'delirious?' concert next week.

John: Oh yeah? Tell me more.

Peter: Well, she said she wouldn't mind coming with me.

John: Great!

Peter: Well, I couldn't help myself. I felt I had to warn her what might happen.

John: Why? Does she have a problem with loud music or something?

Peter: No, not that, but the Christian stuff. Y'know, they talk about God. Sometimes people worship and I thought it might freak her out. So I tried to tell her that she might want to consider becoming a Christian.

John: What happened?

Peter: *Well, she looked at me weird and asked what I was talking about. So I started telling her about sin and everything, but I got all tied up when she asked me what that had to do with a rock concert.*

John: *What happened next?*

Peter: *Well, I thought she really needed to get the right message here, so I remembered what you've always said about keeping Jesus central to things. I told her Jesus died for her, to save her from her sins. She then asked what she'd done wrong and what it had to do with Jesus anyway. I could tell she just wasn't getting it. She was getting awful huffy as well.*

John: *Carry on.*

Peter: *Well, then I told her she had to believe and be baptised. It was at that point she called me a weirdo and walked off! Can you believe it?*

John: *Well, yes, actually I can. I know that you meant well, but you pushed too hard. Sally didn't know what you were talking about and you obviously offended her. That's pretty serious, Peter.*

Peter: *Oh…well, I've heard it said before that the cross is offensive. So isn't that alright?*

John: *The cross of Jesus is offensive because of what it is, because of what happened there, because of the injustice that the perfect son of God should die in my place, when really I deserved it. That's the offence of the cross. You're the offence here Peter. In Sally's eyes you've reduced yourself to a religious bigot. Instead of being her friend, you've become someone who tells her she's wrong.*

Peter: *Yep, I really did blow it didn't I. So what now?*

John: *Well, there's this really helpful little book you might like to read. It's called **'The Art of Connecting'**…*

QUESTION TIME

THREE STORY QUESTION TIME

In three story living you will probably find that you get asked slightly different questions to the usual dilemmas that find you grappling with Christian apologetics. That's not to say you won't have to deal with the likes of: What about all the bad things in the world? What about innocent people suffering? What about creation and evolution? How can you prove God exists? How do you know the Bible is reliable? To explore possible solutions to these kind of questions we would need a lot more time and space than we've got in this book. And besides, they're not what three story living or the art of connecting is all about. So instead, let me point you to a couple of useful websites so you can explore this stuff yourself if you want to:

www.yfc.co.uk
www.talk2.me.uk

You can also get in touch with the Youth For Christ internet pastor, who will help you with specific queries or point you in the right direction so you can find out more. **Contact: www.kev.yfc.co.uk**

The kind of questions and dilemmas you're more likely to face when you're practising the art of connecting are tackled below by National Director of British Youth For Christ, Roy Crowne:

Question: If God's story is so good, why are you one of only a few people I know who believe it?

Actually, out of six billion people on the planet, two billion people do believe it. Look beyond our own doorstep. The truth is that the church is growing throughout the world at a staggering rate. There is a church in North Korea with half a million members and new churches are planted every day in all continents of the world, even if many of them, because of political enforcement, have to be 'underground'. Closer to home, initiatives such as the Alpha Course have seen significant church growth and there are a number of churches in London who regularly meet with congregations of more than two thousand people.

It may be that there are only a few Christians you know about in your school, or perhaps you're part of a relatively small Christian youth group, but the fact that people in your immediate circle of friends don't believe God's story doesn't mean that it is any less true. It just means that those of us who believe it have not communicated it in an effective way.

Dilemma: I think I have pushed my friend too hard and put him off exploring God's story. He doesn't seem to want to talk to me anymore.

Do not kick yourself for this. In the end, God uses all sorts of opportunities and can turn them around for good, even if we make mistakes. There may be other things going on in your friend's life that mean he doesn't want to talk to you. Learn to listen more and try not to impose your own agenda in the future. Suggest a trip to the cinema or something. Just concentrate for now on being a friend. Chill out and don't get wound up about it.

Dilemma: I had the opportunity to speak, but I bottled out.

Sometimes when people ask us questions we just feel embarrassed or uncool. It's natural to feel uncomfortable if you think people might laugh at you. However, you will discover that once you have successfully shared God's story a few times you will become more confident. Remember to share it only when you believe the time is right and be sure to tell it through your own story. It's doubtful that your friends will laugh or criticise. They're probably more interested than you can imagine. Sometimes we just lack confidence, but this is something that you will overcome in time. There will be many more opportunities, so relax and continue to pray that they will come up naturally again when God's timing is right.

Dilemma: I'm scared that I will be talked about if I share my story so openly.

If you have a good relationship with the person you are talking with, this shouldn't happen. However, it is true that in making yourself vulnerable there is the potential for people to laugh or sneer or talk about you. That is sometimes part of what's involved when you stand up for the claims of Christ. It's part of 'taking up your cross'. If you suffer in this way, try to use it to dig deeper into God. The New Testament is full of encouragement for times when we are struggling. Romans 5:3–5, 'We also have joy in our troubles, because we know that these troubles produce patience. And patience produces character, and character produces hope. And this hope will never disappoint us, because God has poured out his love to fill our hearts.' In 1 Thessalonians chapter 2, Paul speaks of the Christian's suffering and the fact that they were insulted by people who were against them. He says, 'But our God helped us to be brave and to tell you his Good News.'

Be encouraged by the fact that your story is out there. You do not know what they will do with the information and knowledge you have given them. Trust the Holy Spirit to continue his work.

Dilemma: I do not think my life matches up to what being a Christian should be.

The important thing is that you have a desire to change and be more like Jesus. Sometimes when you tell your story people have high expectations of what Christians should be like and how they should behave. You need to understand that you are on a journey. Philippians 1:6 tells us, 'God began doing a good work in you, and I am sure he will continue it until it is finished when Jesus Christ comes again.' If part of going public with your faith means you get a closer look into your life and the way it connects to God, that's great. What your friend needs to see is you being genuine, even in your struggles. So keep it real!

Dilemma: I'm sharing my story and some of God's story with my friend but nothing seems to be happening. It seems like he is not interested.

Do not forget that it is God's timing at work here. You never know what is happening to the seed of God's story you have planted in your friend's life. It is God who draws people to Jesus, not you, so just keep praying and persevere.

Dilemma: My friend is going through so much pain and hurt, yet she does not want to hear God's story. I know he could help her if she would only let him.

This is one of the most difficult things, because we know what could happen in our friends' lives if they would only open up to God. All you can do in this situation is continue to care, support and be there for them. This is where your actions will probably communicate more than your words. Perhaps, in the light of this, you can understand more of the way God hurts when we refuse or neglect to turn to him. He is a father who sees his children desperately in need and yet he cannot force us to love him. Yet, rest assured, he will always be there when we are ready to return home.